THE MAN-MADE OBJECT

VISION + VALUE SERIES

THE MAN-MADE OBJECT

EDITED BY GYORGY KEPES

George Braziller, New York

Copyright © 1966 GEORGE BRAZILLER, INC.
All rights reserved.
For information address the publisher:
George Braziller, Inc.
One Park Avenue
New York, New York 10016
Library of Congress Catalog Card number: 66–13046
First Printing
Manufactured in the United States of America

The Origins of Form in Art by Herbert Read
is reprinted from ERANOS-JAHRBUCH XXIX:
MENSCH UND GESTALTUNG, Olga Fröbe-Kapteyn,
editor, Rhein-Verlag, Zurich, 1960.

CONTENTS

Certainly among the prime impulses of man is the impulse *to create objects*. With this term is intended the direct and active manipulation of any matter whatsoever present in our surroundings, thereby bringing into existence some very definite material thing, quite distinct from that which previously existed. The formulation of a general concept which takes in all foreseen and foreseeable cases —be it even as in this instance an essentially "material" concept—is never easy. I shall therefore trust to what follows to develop more fully the exact significance of this term. I want immediately, however, to clarify that in speaking here of the importance invested in "objects" in the panorama of our modern existence, we intend to limit the examination to the whole vast category of "material things" which surround us and which exist for the fact of having been produced, directly or indirectly, by the intervention of man.

I believe one can readily affirm that the object created by man—from the most ancient and prehistoric times—constitutes a kind of extension of man, a manifestation of his very physical, or rather physical-psychical, constitution. The primitive utensil (sharpened flint, hand ax, arrow, knife) or the most refined precision instrument (compass, microscope, transistor) each possesses a twofold aspect: that of being invested with a specific "function" (to wound, to cut, to perform a mechanical operation); and that of "containing," summing up, representing that function by means of an external aspect which has to assume a more or less constant characteristic and which amounts to an "aesthetic" aspect. We are here, perhaps, at the origin of a primitive and still very remote principle of aesthetic functionality, perhaps even more primitive than that which brought one to incise graffiti on the walls of paleolithic caves. I believe it is beyond doubt that a certain degree of "aesthetic pleasure" came into play already in the most ancient objects rediscovered by archaeologists, the objects man has used from the very beginning of his existence on earth. And likewise it is beyond doubt that still today man tends always to invest his objects of common use with some quantity of aesthetic value.

Indeed, both the handmade object and the later industrially produced object are subject to these same basic laws. Here I can only briefly explore this assertion and above all point out the substantial differences between these two categories of objects.[1]

In the handmade object the aesthetic characteristics result from the process of the production itself and can thus be "added," by the "touch" of the artist. In the industrially produced object, on the other hand, every aesthetic quality is already implicit in the design for the object or in the model which will be the matrix of all the successive forms of the series. The production in series of examples all identical is something very particular to our epoch, and something practically unknown in all previous epochs. All handmade products, even when produced with the intervention of a machine, as in the case of some ancient objects produced on a lathe or with an auger, always have a *limit of perfection* and a *margin of chance,* which are unknown to industrially produced objects. This is one of the most notable differences between the two categories of objects. The quantity of objects "made by hand" which can be made much better by machine will always be smaller. In fact, today the handicrafts are destined to become more than anything else a subsidiary of the "pure arts," and to assume those characteristics of preciosity of material and self-sufficiency of form which distinguish painting and sculpture.

Another factor which distinguishes in a singular fashion today's industrially produced object from the old craft object, and likewise from all "artistic objects" of the past as well as of our own day, is the fact that the outdating—the obsolescence of the form—is much more marked in the industrially produced object. In other words, the industrially produced object, for the very fact of its being subject to an accelerated consumption on the part of the masses, sees its formal validity expire at a much faster rate. Indeed the industrially produced object is subject to a rapidity of consumption unknown to other categories of objects and from this results its formal instability. It is this instability that leads to a change which follows the dictates of fashion rather than of style true and proper. Thus the transformation, even very marked transformation, in the forms of the industrially produced objects which surround us, can be completely gratuitous and due excessively to the phenomena of competition, advertising, or sales. That is, they can be subject to the process of "styling" which is so typical of this category of object. But of all this we cannot do more here than make brief mention or we shall go too far from what is the essential core of this discussion.

If, as I have said at the beginning, at one stage the object can be considered as an instrument capable of potentiating and prolonging the operative faculty of the individual, at a second stage the object can be understood as already being—in an autonomous and "pre-existent" sense—part of our surrounding scene. In other terms, those justifications which can have value for the anthropological study of a determined cultural epoch, and which can take into account the emergence and coming into being of the object produced by man "as if before then they had never existed" must, on the other hand, in a study which considers the present state of things, leave place to an evaluation of objects as constituents of a "class in themselves" with which man has a very peculiar rapport. This rapport may be the initial "integrative" one of the object as instrument or prolongation of the person himself, or the "counterpositive" one of the object as "extraneous body," as an element to be appropriated or discarded. And it is above all the object as "extraneous body" that interests us here, because as such it has a closer relationship with the importance assumed by the object in the creation or in the formulation of certain works of art in our day.

Thus, at a certain point the man-made object becomes analogous to that which we can define as the "nature-created object" or natural element spontaneously born but which in the eyes of the spectator can assume the character of an "object." It is easy to give an example of what is meant here: think of the polished stones from the sea, tree trunks, empty bird's nests, or an isolated crystal formation, all of them natural elements which can "function" as objects purposely created, and which, in fact, take on in a work of art—be it as still life or as assemblage—the same function as the "made" object. Such distinctions between man-made or natural objects might seem obvious and simplistic, but they aim only to make more precise how man is constantly surrounded by an immense accumulation of "object elements," in large part created by himself, or created by nature but assumed as if they were "made," and which all together constitute an "external world" from which we derive impulses and pretexts for our formative will—our Gestalt will—in the structuring of works of visual art.

It is not possible here to examine separately all the different categories, subspecies, and families of objects which surround us and by which directly or indirectly our artistic and social panorama is influenced. Because of their particularity, however, I would like at least to point out the presence around us of a notable quantity of objects which have value as "signs," objects, that is, which are "vehicles for signs." Besides the real and actual traffic sign which also carries a most notable importance in the conditioning of our visualization (think of the frequence with which our visual perception is solicited by the form and color of a traffic signal), there exist innumerable other "sign-vehicle" objects which constitute that which we can define as the "urban furnishings," equivalents of the internal furnishings of a house when the city and the urban habitat in general are considered as the ambient scene of our customary life of relations. As soon as we open our minds to this view, we realize that there exists a whole forest of "object elements" which can enter into this category: parking meters, traffic lights, kiosks, telephone poles, mail boxes, rain spouts, water tanks, gas pumps, etc., etc.

All these objects are invested with a significance, almost always institutionalized by use or convention, for which, known and "readable" to us, they would be completely occult and mysterious to individuals from those parts of the world which still escape our mechanized and industrialized civilization. Think of the reaction of a "barbarian" in front of a London mail box which consists of an isolated red cylinder at the edge of the sidewalk; and examples could be multiplied at will. Perhaps many of these objects to the eye of a "barbarian" could take on efficacy similar to that of magical images, ominous, sacred, full of hidden and allegorical meanings, in a certain sense coercive, not very different from the old totemic figures of Polynesia or Africa to our own eyes. Furthermore, many such objects—if one wanted to carry out a psychoanalytic investigation—would reveal sexual-symbolic or phallic, or other such characteristics. Indeed it would be possible and perhaps interesting to do an anthropological study on the distribution according to countries and civilizations of the sexual-symbolic, magical, and other elements in road signals, and in general in the "furnishings" of different cities.

Turning now to an analysis of the value and function of the object in the area of the work of visual art, I must, for the exigencies of space, exclude any consideration of the object *depicted* in painting or sculpture, that is, of the object in still life. Art historians have much debated the possibility of finding the origins of this artistic genre in very distant epochs. But by now the hypothesis is commonly accepted that the true and pure still life, executed only with the intention and the taste of representing a composition of objects (natural or artificial) isolated and by themselves, came into being toward the beginning of the Baroque era. It was therefore during this epoch that man took notice of "things" and objects created by himself as something of such importance as to become "protagonists" of a work of art, taking the place of sacred or historic images. Thus the object at a certain point, supplanting man, became anthropomorphized. The step is very brief from the representing of the object to its "presentation," to its bodily inclusion in the painting. As likewise the step is brief—let us not forget it—to considering the entire work of art (painting, sculpture, mobile, collage, etc.) as an "object" on the same level as a knick-knack or household furnishing.

If from the ingenuous and romantic still life of the nineteenth century we pass to the work of an epoch closer to our own, one of the most singular manifestations to present itself is that of the "glorification of the object" in the work of the Surrealists. This is not the place to repeat the history of a very recent and well known artistic period, but we should here at least recall how the object—henceforth reproduced for the sole end of rendering it more identical to the original—came to acquire some very particular and unusual characteristics, how it came almost to be animated with latent "organic" and at the same time degenerative forces, and how it became animalized and anthropomorphized to the point of giving life to those disturbing oneric objects of Salvador Dalì (think of the liquifying watches, the tumid pianos), and of those multiple sexual-symbolic figurations of René Ma gritte, Max Ernst, and Yves Tanguy, which transport the object, until then immobile, inanimate, and innocuous, into the ambiguous and morbid universe of their paintings. First in the work of the Dadaists and then in that of their successors, the Surrealists, one witnessed for the first time in the history of painting the evaluation of the object as such, with certain "found," isolated, invented, signed, manipulated, and "assembled" objects, emitted for their richness of imagery or for their mythopoetic properties, to serve as works of art in themselves. The examples are, of course, well known and well analyzed in all texts referring to Surrealism.[2)]

Even these very brief remarks are enough to tell us of the importance of the Surrealists' contribution to the "poetics of the object." But what we must analyze here above all are the differences rather than the analogies between the interest imparted to the object by the Surrealists and that which is given to the object by very recent artistic currents, usually indicated with the name Neo-Dadaist.

In the case of the Surrealists, the emission or "assumption" of objects in their works—be it that they reproduce such objects or that they availed themselves of the object directly to construct the work —always had a precise purpose, a purpose which we can define as allegorical, or better, metaphorical. The object thus used was therefore valued above all for its "literary" significance, for its semantic connotation, rather than for its plastic or essential value. The paradoxality of the condition thus created (think of the fur-covered cup of Meret Oppenheim, or the famous *ready-mades* of Marcel Duchamp) readily approached analogous literary experiments (word play, use of puns, metaphors, metonymy, etc.). That such Dadaist and Surrealist objects, once accepted in the museums, labeled, enclosed in glass cases, could assume artistic values that they did not have initially, is something else. And it explains how some ready-mades, now become famous (the bicycle handlebars of Picasso, the *Fountain* of Duchamp), are now idolized as genial formal discoveries, even if originally they were only "literary" juxtapositions, the formal possibilities of which were of a secondary order.

Today things are very different. There exist of course the epigones of Surrealism who still utilize the "found," manipulated, and signed object with the same mentality as their predecessors (a typical example is E. L. T. Mesens), but aside from these the importance and indeed the function of the object in the work of art is now substantially changed, just as the importance of the object in our surroundings is changed in comparison to a few decades ago. I would like now to consider very briefly the function vested in the object in its everyday presence about us, and following this to analyze a bit deeper the situation of the object within those contemporary works of so-called Neo-Dadaist art.

The function of the object in our surroundings is too often treated only from the technical, scientific or, let us say, architectonic point of view, instead of from a rigorously aesthetic point of view. That is, one tends to consider the industrially produced object as a subsidiary product of architecture, while its function and its "position" in our everyday panorama is quite different. Let us see in what this difference consists.

Today, as we have said above, we are surrounded by an inextricable net of "object elements" by which we are in a certain way dominated. The shapes which surround us are no longer, as they once were, limited almost exclusively to those produced in the current era and therefore bound to one definite stylistic formulation. Rather, we are immersed, in our dwellings and museums, within a wide stream of objects coming from the most distant cultural epochs: Minoan and Aztec amphorae, Cycladic and Etruscan statuettes, Chinese porcelain and Medieval plate, Baroque and Art Nouveau furniture, and beyond this we continually use objects furnished by industry and subject to the laws of styling and redesign, which continually change their forms at very brief intervals of time.

We handle or see about us ball-point pens, paper-cutters, clocks, books, eyeglasses, refrigerators, scooters, jets, pots, etc., all of which doubtless condition us in an almost absolute manner toward a certain formal orientation. So complete is this conditioning that only with great difficulty can we conceive the existence of forms different from those to which we are accustomed. But—and here lies the core of the problem—with the immense diffusion of mass production, objects similar or identical one to the other are more numerous than those different from one another. In other words, our glances are struck above all by objects of a standardized type. This fact necessarily gives rise to two phenomena which are opposed to each other, but which in point of fact are equivalent—phenomena to which I have frequently alluded[3] because they seem to me to be determinative for the aesthetic structure of our age.

The first of these two phenomena consists in that which I would like to define "formal conformity": the equalizing and leveling of ubiquitous *vis formativa* which leads to a leveling of creative fantasy and to a world-wide acceptance of certain champion-forms.

The second phenomenon, directly bound and at the same time in opposition to the first, is the reaction to this equalizing and leveling, a reaction which consists in gratuitously redesigning or re-styling objects for the sole purpose of making a stronger impression on the consumer and inducing him to buy. Exceptional forms are thus conceived and constructed, exclusively or at least principally for the reason of rendering them more evident and spectacular. And this in turn leads to a devaluation of the intrinsic value of the form itself. This does not mean that today there are not objects equally "beautiful"—the forms of which are equally "pure" and "eurhythmic"—as in the remote past, but it does mean that this happens very rarely, and exactly because of this necessity on the part of the producer to modify the form of the object, even when this form already can respond to every practical and functional demand, only to facilitate its sale.

Thus today as never before, the object is universalized: all over the world men come in contact with objects analogous except for small national differences which are always diminishing and are limited to minimal particulars. And yet think of the enormous impact of the presence of foreign objects to which we are not accustomed. Think of the extraordinary importance in creating the atmosphere of a country that the presence of certain forms and colors belonging to that country have. In this connection these forms and colors, which above we defined as the "urban furnishings," have an importance greater than the architecture of a country and almost greater than the physical nature of a land. Think of the effect of the red double-decker bus of London, of the particular type of billboards in Switzerland, of the fire escapes in Chicago or other American cities, of the form and color and type of cigarette packaging, canned foods, bottles of beer, wine flasks, etc. All this indicates the immense influence which the formal element constituting the object of everyday use has on us, and also how as differentiating element the man-made object is almost stronger than the natural elements of the landscape.

Must we then consider as near, the end of this very particular differentiation between the countries of the earth? We can respond affirmatively regarding the rapid generalization of the technical structure and the universalizing of the use of the major part of the objects; but negatively in light of the equally rapid changing of the prototypes created by industrial design due precisely to the process of obsolescences. And this explains why today we are witnessing a new phenomenon: the urgency on the part of man to "fix" certain objects of common use and to avail himself of them as provocators of works of art; to introduce into the work of sculpture or painting elements taken from daily life almost as if to halt their transitoriness. At the base of this fact I believe are to be recognized very profound reasons, still not well investigated. There is no doubt, for example, that the "taste" of the masses is today more than yesterday based on the presence around us of a tide of mass-produced elements. I refer, for example, to television programs, advertising, industrially produced objects. The presence, very nearly coercive, of all these elements is indisputably responsible for the particular formation of our taste. And indeed, as Harold Rosenberg has affirmed,[4] it is likely that the usual devaluation of such objects of *Kitsch* is completely erroneous; it is instead in just these objects that we must discover some of the fundamental aesthetic "constants" of our epoch. The best proof of this is to be had in the fact that the most refined and accomplished artists make use of such elements, "incorporating" them in their work, be it as collages (from Kurt Schwitters to Robert Rauschenberg), be it by "copying" or reproducing by hand common industrially produced objects (Jasper Johns, Roy Lichtenstein).

The other fundamental reason for the utilization for an artistic end of industrially produced objects and in general of products commonly found on the market, must be discovered in a precise will to "mythicize"[5] exactly the elements used by the masses. This is a phenomenon which I believe has never been encountered in an epoch previous to our own. Indeed, can we not consider as deriving from an analogous principle the archaeological orientation of our contemporary culture? The present tendency to "fetishize" the excavated object, the most humble instrument discovered as a result of historical or archaeological investigations, and to raise it to the dignity and value of a work of art, most of the time only in virtue of its archaicness, must make us reflect seriously. At this rate, could it not be asserted that in a distant—and yet not too distant—future, one might see conserved in museums objects belonging to our civilization, the exact mechanical understanding of which will by then have been lost, while the objects themselves will be considered not as "technical" prototypes of successively developed mechanisms, but rather conserved and "idolatrized" exactly for their formal-aesthetic quality? We can easily imagine fragments of old steam engines, rusted gears of turbines or electric trains, minute elements of old transistors or of "electronic brains" religiously kept within glass cases, and considered important "pieces," precious testimony of twentieth-century art. The idea is quite other than impossible or improbable. Furthermore, we must confess that already today visiting the rooms of some museums of technology that house old machines of the last century, we cannot but experience, in front of such relics, a sensation of aesthetic pleasure, very near to that which we experience before certain contemporary works of art which make use of mechanical fragments, such as those of Eduardo Paolozzi, John Chamberlain, César, David Smith, etc.

All these works constructed with materials taken from modern technology or actually incorporating mechanical objects or their fragments exhibit the will to join to the creation of the work of art elements typical of our cultural season, extracting from it plastic images. Unfortunately, there is another factor which must be taken into account in examining such works, and this is the negative—fetishizing—element which often risks compromising the value of these works and which, in my opinion, decrees their limits.

At this point a parenthesis seems necessary, otherwise it will be impossible to penetrate the mechanisms which regale this "aesthetic transference" of values of the object of common use to those of the artistic object. A particularity of our epoch—especially in countries of very high economic development, but rapidly extending everywhere—is the habit and the impulse to "throw away," to get rid of the objects which surround us even before they have been thoroughly used. This tendency, which clearly originates from precise economic conditions and which therefore rests on precise and firm laws of the market, insinuates in a decisive manner on our whole way of being and conceiving life and art. In place of a gradual flow of fashion and style—which was to be noted up through the last century—there has taken over a rapid succession of tastes, at times founded upon definitely functional and rational motives, but most of the time due almost exclusively to the urgency of the changes to which man is subjected, urgency which is abetted and increased by able advertising and the marketing of always newly created products. But—and here we touch specifically the problem we are treating—it happens that in direct contrast with the impulse to *throw away the ordinary object* there is being established an acute need to *treasure the ephemeral,* to collect and value the transitory, and in this case not for practical-economic reasons, but rather for symbolic-allegorical ones.

This then is how, and why we are witnessing the creation of "artistic objects" by incorporating and transforming as raw material for construction the object which otherwise would have been destroyed or thrown on the rubbish heap. Such objects thus come to acquire a value, symbolic both in respect to the world from which they are taken, and as representation, or better, as privileged "presentation" of themselves.

The "combine paintings" of Rauschenberg, and after him of Fernandez Arman, Daniel Spoerri, Martial Raisse, and of the whole band of creators of assemblages, are compositions only in appearance animated by the spirit of the old Dada. Only in appearance because in these "conglomerations" various objects, among the most banal (Coca Cola bottles, milk cartons, fragments of rotogravure, etc.) or the most exceptional (stuffed birds, feathers, sponges, crystals), are brought together without a nihilist or blasphemist will, but rather through a clever pictorial utilization of single elements, assumed just as much for their compositional and structural value as for their evocative and mythopoetic value. In fact, the Coca Cola bottle, the glass, the portrait of Eisenhower, as such, destined for the trash heap, once "fixed" within the painting continue to live, filled with their associative value, evocators of particular atmospheres, states of mind, memories. And furthermore, it is possible that they will continue to have value as provocators of images for just their formal and formative quality, even once they have partially or totally lost the "semantic aura" with which they are today impregnated. It has in fact been demonstrated[6] that even in the case of the ancient artistic object, the work of art of other epochs bound to precise cultic and initiatic motives, the vitality of the symbols used was able to endure, even when the "conceptual" knowledge of such symbols and their historic or religious significance had been lost; this was so precisely because of the "transconceptual" and essentially iconic quality of those symbols.

If then one were to say that the duration of these objects included in works of art today, or indeed the chronological duration of the whole work of art based on these "object elements," is destined to be quite brief and is indeed bound to the recognizability of the objects in their context, I would not repudiate this. Not all art of all times is destined to an unlimited duration, to a hypothetical "eternity." It can well be that this kind of art of our day, bound to the object and to its transitoriness, must also itself be transitory and fleeting like the object from which it derives its formative origin. This would still not contradict the possibility of admitting the existence and validity of this art for our own day.

In concluding this introductory discussion I should like to restate, above all, the importance of the object in our era, not only aesthetic, but sociological and anthropological as well. I have tried to demonstrate here how in our contemporary world there has been a notable dilation of the object panorama. The consequences of this fact are evident in the insertion of the object into the work of art, and in the impact that the object as such has on the individual and on society. We have also noted the importance which the formal element present in the objects which surround us can have in the formation of taste and customs, and we have reviewed the advantages and dangers inherent in the phenomenon of obsolescence of forms which we are presently witnessing.

Only the future can tell if our era has known how to express, through the objects it has produced, a greater or lesser creative vitality in comparison with previous eras. Yet—if I am allowed a declaration of faith in man and in his inventive faculty—I believe that our civilization is about to demonstrate that, in spite of the incredible transformations due to the end of the crafts and to the advent of an almost total mechanization, man has not lost, and is probably not destined to lose in the future, his creative and imaginative capacity, but he has perhaps even augmented and perfected it.

1. *Cf.* G. Dorfles, *Simbolo, Comunicazione, Consumo,* Turin, Einaudi (1962).
2. *Cf.* Jean Marcel, *Histoire du Surréalisme,* Paris, Editions du Seuil (1959), Chapter VIII.
3. *Cf.* G. Dorfles, *Divenire delle arti,* Turin, Einaudi (1958).
4. Harold Rosenberg, *The Tradition of the New,* New York, Grove Press (1961).
5. G. Dorfles, *Nuovi riti, nouvi miti,* Turin, Einaudi (1965).
6. *Cf.* G. Dorfles, *Le oscillazioni del gusto,* Milan, Lerici (1958).

OBJECT FORMS AND FUNCTIONS: CONTRASTS AND ANALOGIES

Railroad station coal stove.
Photo courtesy Standard Oil.

Two-oven electric range.
Photo courtesy Frigidaire.

12

Shaman's copper rattle, from Alaska.
Peabody Museum, Harvard University.

Portable TV set. Photo courtesy Zenith.

14

Pueblo pottery, from New Mexico, *circa* A.D. 1200.
Peabody Museum, Harvard University.

Blown and molded glass vases. Designed by Flavio
Poli and produced by Seguso Vetri d'Arte, Murano.

Pre-Columbian pottery plate from Panama.
Peabody Museum, Harvard University.

Trays of silvered nickel. Designed by Lino
Sabattini and produced by Cristofle, Milan.

Shell mask from Lick Creek Mound, Tennessee.
Peabody Museum, Harvard University.

Bronze bell, Japanese, second century B.C.–first century A.D.
Museum of Fine Arts, Boston.

Alarm clock. Designed by Rodolfo Bonetto and produced by Flli. Borletti, Milan.

Dictating equipment by IBM. Photo Ezra Stroller.

Arrowhead, Chinese, Shang period, *circa* 1700 B.C.
Peabody Museum, Harvard University.

Ballpoint pen. Photo courtesy Parker Pen Company.

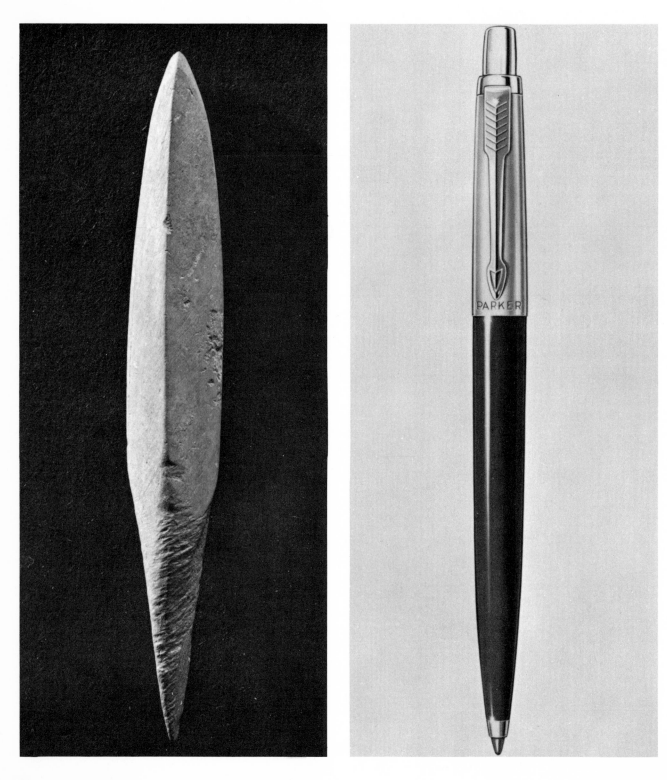

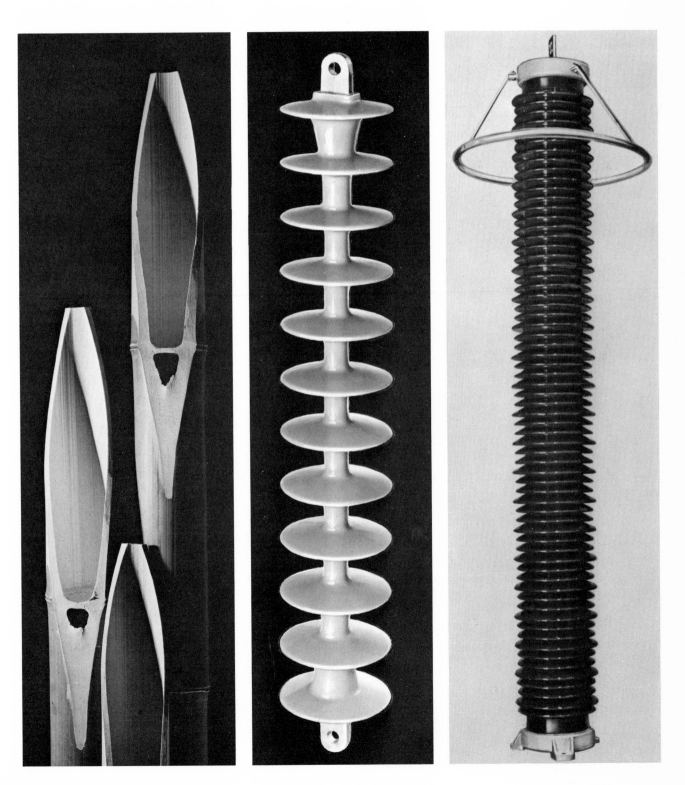

Tenement of objects.

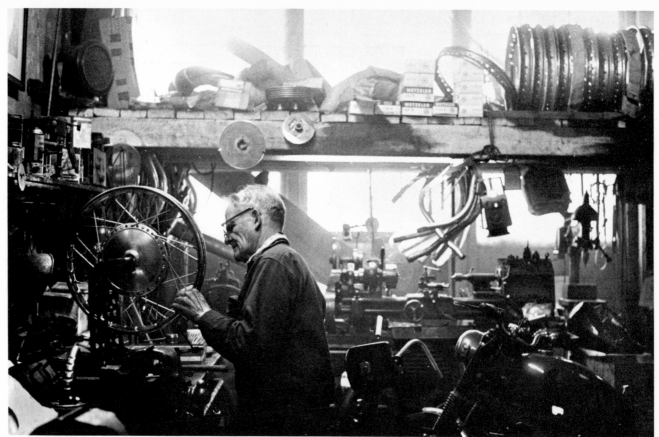

Object hospital.

Car cemetery.

Furnishings of a Shaker room.

26

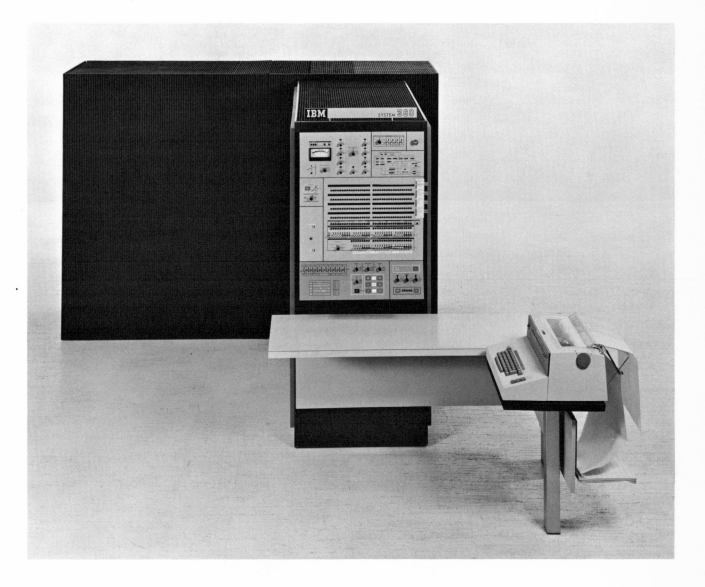

IBM System 360 installation.

Form in art is the shape imparted to an artifact by human intention and action. In English "form" seems to have an aesthetic connotation not carried by the word "shape," but shape, which is cognate with the Old English *sceapan* and the German *schaffen,* better conveys the creative implications of this human activity. Form is also given to natural objects, either by the process of growth, or by crystallization of other physical changes, and there is a whole science of form in nature which we call morphology, after the Greek word for form. But there is no distinct science dealing with form in human artifacts, though these have distinctive laws or habits of perfection.

Form, as I shall discuss it, must be distinguished from composition. I shall not be concerned with the relation of parts to a whole, or to the laws of harmony and proportion that govern their interrelations. Of course, every form can be measured, and one can discuss the harmonic significance of these measurements, or their lack of harmony. But the interesting problem, and one to which practically no attention has ever been directed, is the origins of the very concept of form in art. Why, out of the shapeless chaos of sticks and stones, or out of the handy and useful objects which were the first tools of primitive man, did form progressively emerge until it surpassed the utilitarian purpose of the formed object and became a form for the sake of form, that is to say, a work of art?

I am, perhaps, already begging the question, but I will clarify it by some precise illustrations from the artifacts of prehistoric man. Man is first differentiated in the process of evolution by an ability to make tools. It has been proved by Professor Wolfgang Köhler in his famous experiments with chimpanzees that apes are capable of improvising tools, but this only happens when the animal is incited by the prospect of a *visible* reward. The ape lacks two components of thought upon which man's toolmaking depends: the power of combining mental images—in short, imagination—and the power of speech and the conceptual process that result from speech. This is perhaps not immediately obvious, but Dr. Kenneth Oakley of the British Museum of Natural History has recently reduced the considerable research on this subject to the following cautious statement:

> One may sum up by saying that apes of the present day are capable of perceiving the solution of a visible problem, and occasionally of improvising a tool to meet a given situation; but to conceive the idea of shaping a stone or a stick for use in an imagined future eventuality is beyond the mental capacity of any known apes. Possession of a great capacity for this conceptual thinking, in contrast to the mainly perceptual thinking of apes and other primates, is generally regarded by comparative psychologists as distinctive of man. Systematic making of tools implies a marked capacity for conceptual thought.[1]

The recent experiments in training chimpanzees to paint do not contradict such a conclusion. Congo, the chimpanzee in the London Zoo trained by Dr. Desmond Morris,[2] did produce amazingly effective paintings, but not only were the colors preselected by the scientist in charge of the experiments, but they were presented to the chimpanzee one by one, and the paper on which he painted was usually withdrawn to allow each color to dry separately, and so safeguard against any accidental tendency to mix the colors. The design is due to a combination of random muscular actions and automatic perceptual processes—a "good Gestalt" may result, as indeed it does from various automatic painting machines that have been invented during recent years. But again, there is no capability of combining images, no shaping power of the imagination.

If we turn now to the first objects deliberately shaped by man, which are tools of various kinds, we find a chronological sequence which begins with convenient pieces of sharp stone, sharks' teeth or shells, anything with a cutting edge, and gradually (over many thousands of years) leads to objects deliberately shaped for this purpose.[3] The earliest tools are known as eoliths (dawn stones) and are indistinguishable from the accidents of nature. Such stones are still used by Australian tribes. The problem of distinguishing these eoliths from deliberately shaped tools need not concern us: we may merely note that there gradually appear various types of stone implements that are unmistakably shaped by human agency. Usually of flint, they have been produced by flaking the natural stone. The flint is sharply tapped at a point on the surface with the result that a flake of a certain size is chipped off, and by progressive blows at the right points, the required shape is produced—the shape required by the function of the tool. The process could give two possible end results: the flake that was removed from the flint, and the core of flint from which flakes had been removed. Either might be utilized as a tool, the flake as a scraper, for example, and the core as a hand ax.

Once the process had been invented, then the way was open for a continuous refinement of skill and of the tools produced by the skill, this process of refinement going hand-in-hand with the choice of more effective materials and the invention of new methods of working. It should be realized, however, that an immense period of time stretches between the earliest appearance of the pear-shaped hand ax, the distinctive tool of the Lower Paleolithic period in Europe (*ca.* 550,000 to 250,000 years ago) and the invention of the refined tools of the Neolithic period (*ca.* 3000 to 2000 B.C.). Something like half

1. Paleolithic flint hand axes.
American Museum of Natural History, New York.

2. Neolithic flint knives from Denmark.
American Museum of Natural History, New York.

a million years of experience in stone precedes the swift elaboration of iron and bronze. But once iron had replaced stone, and bronze had replaced (or been added to) iron, man had at his command the technical means for the establishment of an enduring civilization.

In order to get a clearer idea of the formal or morphological evolution of these artifacts, it would be best to divide them into three types: 1) piercing and cutting implements, where sharpness is the guiding motive; 2) hammering or bludgeoning implements, where concentrated mass and power is the purpose; and 3) hollow vessels to be used as containers of a food. We shall then find that although the purposes are different, the morphological evolution proceeds along parallel lines.

There can be no possible doubt that for long periods of time the drive behind such evolution was for efficiency. There can equally be no doubt that the search for efficiency led imperceptibly to forms which were not only efficient, but also, for our modern sensibility, beautiful. In any long sequence of axheads or spearheads or arrowheads there is a progressive refinement of shape due to increasing skill in flaking, then in abrading and polishing, until finally we have artifacts of such elegance that it is not reasonable to suppose they could have been intended as practical tools. Archaeologists distinguish between several Paleolithic cultures on the basis of the prevailing tools—for example, pebble-tool and hand-ax cultures, chopper-tool cultures, flake-tool and blade-tool cultures—but I do not think these need concern us, because whatever the tool, and whatever the material, the process of refinement was the same. We must not exclude, of course, the possibility of periods of degeneration.

What I would like to establish, for all these early human artifacts, is an evolutionary sequence that passes through three stages: 1) conception of the object as a tool; 2) making and refinement of the tool to a point of maximum efficiency; 3) refinement of the tool beyond the point of maximum efficiency towards a conception of form-in-itself. The evolution from the first to the second stage is not in doubt; it is the normal cultural sequence as established by paleontologists and archaeologists. But in what manner, and for what reason, did man quite early in his cultural development, and long before historical times, pass from functional form to form-in-itself, that is to say, to aesthetic form?

There are two possible hypotheses that might lead us toward an explanation of the origins of aesthetic form. The first might be called *naturalistic* or *mimetic*, the second, perhaps *idealistic*. According to the first hypothesis, all formal deviations from efficiency would be due to the imitation, conscious or unconscious, of forms found in nature; according to the second hypothesis, form has its own significance, that is to say, corresponds to some inner psychic necessity, and is expressive of this feeling. Such feeling is not necessarily indeterminate; on the contrary, it is often a desire for reification, clarification, precision, order.

3a. Flint dagger from Denmark. Neolithic, *circa* 1500–1200 B.C. British Museum, London.

3b. Jade ritual halberd blade. Chinese, before 1000 B.C. British Museum, London.

3c. Jade ritual halberd blade. Chinese, Shang-Ying period, 1766–1122 B.C. British Museum, London.

3d. Jade ritual blade. Chinese, Chou Dynasty, 1122–247 B.C. The Metropolitan Museum of Art, New York.

3a   3b   3c   3d

Let us now look a little more closely at some of the first human artifacts, and let us take, for the sake of contrast, a solid cutting form, such as the axhead, and a hollow containing form, such as the clay vessel.

The first stages in the formal development of the axhead were obviously pragmatic—a selection of the stone for size and compactness, for striking power consistent with handiness. Important, too, at a later stage of development, was an ovoid shape that permitted the attachment of the head to a shaft by means of thongs. But once this basic form had been standardized by a process of trial and correction, then the toolmaker began to concentrate on the cutting power of the ax, and this led to a gradual refinement of the flaking technique, and then to smoothing and polishing by various methods of abrasion. What was finally evolved, allowing for differences due to the nature of the material, was a shape essentially the same as the ax of civilized man. In all tool design there is an optimum point of functional efficiency which determines shape in the terms of the material used. In many of his artifacts—spear and arrowheads, scrapers, blades, as well as axes—man reached this optimum point in the Late or Upper Paleolithic period.

Then began the final and most significant stage of formal evolution, which does not take place before the Mesolithic period or Middle Stone Age, perhaps not before the Neolithic period: the ax was divorced from its utilitarian function, and further refined to serve as a ritual or ceremonial object. At this stage even the original material, which for a practical tool had to be as strong as possible, was sometimes abandoned, and instead a rare and precious material, such as jadite, was substituted. Jadite and nephrite are hard stones, and were undoubtedly used for the making of tools before such tools became ritualistic or ceremonial objects; and stone or bronze tools also became ritualistic or ceremonial objects where jadite and nephrite were scarce or unknown. But scarcity leads to preciousness, to scarcity values, and for this reason we may suppose that where it was available, notably in China, jadite or nephrite was preferred for nonutilitarian objects. In any case, form, having become divorced from function, was free to develop according to new principles or laws—those laws and principles which we now call aesthetic.

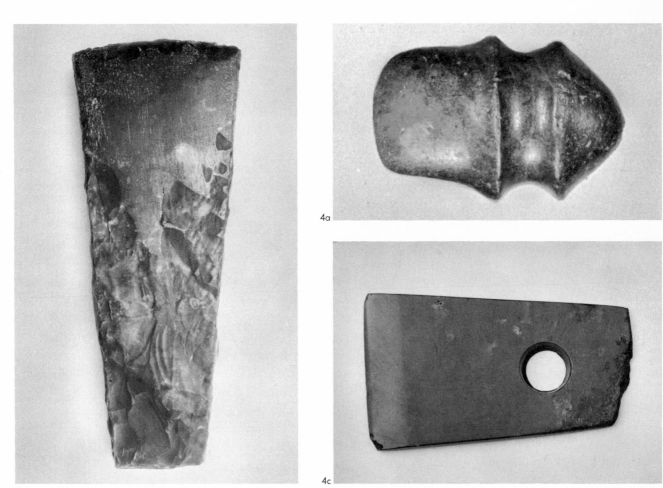

4a. Flint ax. Denmark, Neolithic period.
American Museum of Natural History, New York.

4b. Flint ax. Denmark, Neolithic period.
American Museum of Natural History, New York.

4c. Nephrite ax. Chinese, Neolithic period.
The Metropolitan Museum of Art, New York.

Archaeologists may differ in the classification of prehistoric stone implements—there is naturally a large intermediate group which may be refined functional forms or equally free aesthetic forms, but no archaeologist will deny the general line of development. But it is not essential to find a ritualistic justification for every aesthetic form; there are arrowheads, for example, of extraordinary grace and refinement, which were certainly weapons of the chase, and in no sense ritualistic. It must be admitted that "a purely aesthetic principle of elegance" can be combined with, and be indistinguishable from, a purely utilitarian principle of efficiency. Symmetry, for example, an aesthetic quality when man is conscious of it, was undoubtedly at first a technical necessity: an asymmetrical arrowhead would not fly straight. The problem is to determine at what point elegance ceases to be utilitarian, at what point form is divorced from function.

The ceremonial ax, which has its origins in the Late Stone Age, is highly elaborated in the Bronze Age and then persists throughout most cultures down to the Middle Ages in Europe. This artifact, in its refined stages of development, became a symbolic form. Magnificent bronze axes, which can scarcely have been real weapons, were common in ancient China. Dr. Gunnar Andersson states that the ax was one of the symbols of fertility in the Neolithic period, and compares to it the hammer which Tori laid on the knees of the bride.[4] Jade axheads of the Chou period were certainly cult objects. In the Minoan civilization the double-bladed ax (the *labyris*) was associated with whatever cult was practiced in the labyrinth (to which it gave its name). Placed within a circle (for example, between the curved horns of an ox) it becomes a mandala. In later civilizations we find the ax used as a symbol of authority in, for example, the Roman *fasces,* and its symbolic function persists in the ceremonial halberds of the Medieval and Renaissance pageants. Parallels can be found in Mexican and African cultures. But it is not the historical continuity of the form that is of immediate interest, but the nature of the form that guarantees such continuity.

A similar development with even longer continuity can be traced from the Stone Age hammer to the mace, which is still the symbol of royal and parliamentary authority in several countries. Some authorities[5] suggest that the Chinese *pi,* a jade disk varying considerably in size, generally between 10 and 20 cm. in diameter, and pierced in the center with a circular hole, was derived from the Neolithic mace—a stone mace has been found on a Neolithic site in Mongolia. The pi symbolizes heaven and was used in sacrificial ceremonies. It was also a token of rank and one of the emblematic objects used in burial rites.

4d. Jade ritual ax. Chinese, Chou Dynasty, 1122–247 B.C. The Metropolitan Museum of Art, New York.

4d

5a. Stone mace head from Tell Agrab.
Mesopotamian, *circa* 2800 B.C.
The Metropolitan Museum of Art, New York.

5b. Stone mace head dedicated to the God
Mes-lam-Ta-E-A. Babylonian, *circa* 2500 B.C.
British Museum, London.

5c. Votive hammer head dedicated to the
God Nergal. Babylonian, *circa* 2500 B.C.
British Museum, London.

5d. Jade disk (*pi*). Chinese, Neolithic period.
British Museum, London.

39

The evolution of the hollow vessel is even more interesting and complicated. The first vessels were small pieces of rock with one surface concave enough to hold a liquid. Use must also have been made of gourds, coconut shells, fish shells, and other natural objects; and the progress of cutting the scraping tools must have made possible the hollowing of wood.

With the transition from hunting to agriculture, the possibility of working new materials was discovered, and in particular the plastic virtues of the soil which had become the source of man's basic food, grain. Max Raphael, one of the few archaeologists who has given any thought to the problem of form, in his work on prehistoric Egyptian pottery, gives this account of the origins of the clay vessel:

> Man sought unceasingly for new materials, techniques, and ideologies by which to develop his creative abilities in the face of superior natural forces. The alluviated ground, the nature of which remained a mystery to him, produced what he needed by dint of unremitting labour that entailed a number of equally mysterious and unknown changes beyond the control of man . . .
>
> Because of this complex interaction of necessity and creative power man looked upon the products of this soil, the periodic harvests of barley and wheat that could not be increased at will, with feelings that neither the fruit gatherers nor the hunters had ever experienced—that is, with a desire to store them providentially for future security. Thus with the boom of harvests there was born the need for vessels impervious to moisture and sand, receptacles that could protect the fruits of nature and man's labour from decay.[6]

The possibility of molding clay was eventually discovered, and of baking it in the sun or embers:

> Experience taught the Neolithic Egyptian that the silt from which the grain grew was pliant and plastic, that the sun dried it and made it serviceable as a container, and that firing made it impervious to water. The man who synthetized these separate experiences invented the clay vessel. And in thereby satisfying one of the most urgent social needs, he raised the spiritual value of the material that not only served the growth of grain but also made possible the preservation of it. Man saw that his entire existence depended upon a substance whose origin and nature he did not understand and which he could not produce himself.[7]

But the Neolithic Egyptian could give form to this mysterious substance. The first vessels were round semispherical bowls, but the nature of the material inspired variations from the beginning— bowls with low walls became platters, bowls with high walls became beakers and grain urns. Then came the desire to cover the bowl, for better containment of the liquid, for better protection from flies, and to mold its shape for better pouring or for carrying—each need calling forth an adaptation of the prototype. And again the process of refinement of the basic utilitarian shape set in, and here one must suppose that certain affinities with the shape of the human body had an unconscious influence. Symmetry was imposed by the need for balance, and for the same reason a foot or base was differentiated. The need to lift and transport the larger vessels led to the addition of lugs or handles, but always at some point in the evolution of the utilitarian shape, utility is exceeded. The form is refined for its own sake, or for the sake of a function that is no longer strictly utilitarian. The vessel may be used for libations, for holding grain or the ashes of the dead; and such ritualistic functions can justify refinements not required for normal use. What is essential to note is that at some point in this process of formal evolution the form responds, not only to a utilitarian purpose, but also to a spiritual need.

The important point to realize is that (again in Max Raphael's words) "the fashioning of clay went beyond gratification of physical needs." And Raphael makes the further subtle point that "this development was favoured by the fact (erroneously regarded by many writers as a limitation) that the human hand could produce the synthesis between utilitarian and spiritual purposefulness without resort to any tool."

We must still ask by what forces, and under what guiding will, did the utilitarian shapes of the first clay vessels become the refined forms of later cultures? Max Raphael, who was a dialectical materialist by philosophical conviction, believed that the forces were economic—new needs, often imported by invading races who transformed the old conditions of life.

Max Raphael argues that when the material conditions change, man's emotional reactions change, among these his aesthetic reactions. The old forms no longer satisfy the new feelings: they must be modified to correspond to an inner necessity, a will to form which is an emotional reaction to life as a whole—"the totality of all interacting objective conditions," as he calls it. This seems to imply that there was an evolving consciousness of form as such.

> When Neolithic man, motivated perhaps by the practical purpose of achieving greater imperviousness to liquids, combined polishing with painting and applied both to a form he had created, his consciousness of freedom was increased. The new means of representation changed the impression produced by the pot, and the man consequently gained insight regarding the difference between the actual nature and the effect of a given form. Formerly, when the prehistoric artist for the first time applied mathematics to matter, the effect was only an outward adjustment—the weight of the material, despite its smoothness, still opposed the abstraction of mathematics. Now, when polished color concealed the material from the eye, the mind began to play with the impression of gravitational pull and tried to eliminate it. This tendency was heightened by the fact that the material was actually reduced to a fairly thin layer. In the much-admired thinness of Bavarian pottery we are confronted not only with virtuosity (which surely must have had a high market value), not only with the purely aesthetic principle of elegance, but with a general ideological force that attempted to play with the opposition between matter and spirit, that is, endeavoured to stress or to eliminate this opposition by dematerializing the material and materializing the immaterial.[8]

Here we have a formula for the power that transforms a utilitarian shape into a work of art—an ideological power that *plays* with the opposition between spirit and matter and endeavors to eliminate this opposition. Before we consider the adequacy of this formula, which might be illustrated even more strikingly by tracing the evolution of the bronze vessel in Neolithic China, let us glance at the origins of form in pictorial art.

We have established three stages in the development of the shape of objects of utility—namely, 1) discovery of the functional form, 2) refinement of the functional form to its maximum efficiency, and

3) refinement of the functional form in the direction of free or symbolic form. To suppose a priori that pictorial art, the art of representing images, underwent similar stages of development would perhaps be unwarranted. It is, of course, just possible that the first depictions of animals had a utilitarian purpose—a tally system for huntings or killings—but before the art of drawing could reach the value of a representational symbol, there must have been a long process of development, upward from aimless scratching or scribbling in sand or on the damp clayey walls of the caves. Scribbles and the outlined silhouettes of hands have survived in various Paleolithic sites, and though there is no stratographical evidence to constitute an evolutionary development from aimless scribbling to the representational image or schema, the analogy of the similar development of pictorial representation in the drawings of children is perhaps admissible. But this is not the random activity ending in an accidental discovery of resemblances that a superficial observation might lead one to suppose it to be. Patient analysis of the scribbling activity in children, such as that conducted by Mrs. Rhoda Kellogg among infants in San Francisco, shows that there is a progressive discovery of basic forms—the circle, the cross, the square, and so on—all tending toward a synthetic form which is our old friend, the mandala—a circle divided into four sections. This mandala constitutes a basic schema from which images are developed by the process already mentioned which Professor Gombrich has called "making and matching"[9]—that is to say, the schema is gradually modified in the direction of the retinal image, until a convincing approximation is achieved. On this hypothesis it can be maintained that "what the artist knows" (the schema) is gradually modified by "what the artist sees" (the illusion of reality) and that this process accounts for all variations of style in the history of representational art.

From this point of view chance rock formations or protuberances on the wall of the cave might have served as schemas for Paleolithic man, but this is a phenomenon that occurs most frequently at the peak of Franco-Cantabrian art. Paolo Graziosi, in the latest and most comprehensive survey of Paleolithic art, comes to the conclusion that "nothing so far proves that fortuitous realism acted as a dominant creative impulse in the earliest forms of art"—on the contrary, "it flourished especially in those who had attained a high degree of sensitivity in form and volume, and a remarkable mastery of technical skills."[10]

It is reasonable to suppose, however, that casual scratches and scribbles may have suggested a mental schema to which the deliberate drawing was then matched—or equally probably, there may have been a gradual attempt to match the scribble to the eidetic image. But the more successful the attempt, the less interesting it becomes from a formal point of view: the reproduction of an eidetic image, however life-like, is not necessarily a work of art. It is an illustration and only becomes a work of art if there is an intention to compose or arrange the image in a significant form. The exact illustration of a reindeer or a rhinoceros corresponds to the tool of maximum efficiency. To constitute an artistic form the illustration must be carried beyond this utilitarian stage towards a conception of pure form. Or, to put the same thought in another way: the exact representation of an animal is a reproduction of natural form; we are concerned with forms deliberately conceived by the human imagination.

It has been suggested by some archaeologists that certain of the drawings of animals at Altamira are deliberately composed in this manner: they have "style" as well as "exactitude." But a categorical distinction must be made between "style" and "form." Style corresponds to vitality, to kinetic qualities; form to beauty, to static qualities. Style is human, and limited to human artifacts; form is universal, and exists only when human artifacts correspond to mathematical laws. In general we may say that the Paleolithic artist achieved style but was not aware of form.

We still lack, however, a convincing explanation of why, so early in human development, the approximation of image to reality should have been achieved with such efficiency, though only in one category—the representation of animals. That explanation, it seems to me, must be sought in the social structure that conditioned the production of the images—that is to say, in the very precise requirements of the magical practices of Paleolithic man. I have suggested also that it would be legitimate to suppose at this early stage of human development, a constitutional acuteness of imagery in the human brain—that is to say, a prevailing *eidetic* imagery such as children and certain animals may possess. But if children possess such images, why do they not also produce drawings of similar realistic accuracy? I think one can say: because they have no compelling motive such as the fear and hunger that through a long period of development drove prehistoric man to the institution and elaboration of sympathetic magic.

It is obvious that between any preliminary scribbling stage in the development of prehistoric representational art and the attainment of realistic imagery there once more intervened a will, and though in this case the will did not work upon a utilitarian shape, a tool, it nevertheless took a given form—the basic scribble form—and transformed it with some deliberate intention. We must suppose that the basic form—the mandala—had been achieved by an unconscious will—we may, if we wish to remain materialistic up to this point, suppose that it is no more than a perceptual process that automatically, by reason of perceptual ease and balance, achieves the good Gestalt. But the modification of the basic form then proceeds by an equally perceptual process of making and matching to a point where the illusion of realism is achieved. This stage we may regard as equivalent to the elaboration of the perfectly functional tool—the realistic image is a tool required by sympathetic magic. But then, perhaps in some of the Paleolithic drawings at Altamira, but more obviously in the carved amulets of the female figure such as the Venuses of Lespuge (France) and Dolní Vestoniče (Mikulov District of Moravia) formalization approaches abstraction. There intervenes a will to form that carries the image beyond its utilitarian function and beyond even its stylistic vitality, to constitute once again *free* or *symbolic form*. What takes place is an elaboration of the realistic or utilitarian image, and a gradual substitution, for this image, of a shape that has a power of attraction, and of satisfaction, that proceeds from the shape itself and not from its perceptual or representational function.[11]

It would seem, therefore, that in whatever direction we investigate the origins of form, we see the emergence of an independent will to form, which usually begins to manifest itself when the functional efficiency of the form has reached its optimum point of development and has then become stabilized. We still have no adequate conception of the causation of this will, nor indeed of its teleological justification. Is it merely, as some aestheticians have supposed, a playful impulse to elegant variation; or can it possess a motivation in terms of man's biological evolution? I assume that within the term "biological evolution" we must be prepared to include the development of those faculties by means of which man achieves a mental, that is to say, a spiritual, adjustment to the mystery of his existential situation—a means of answering what Heidegger has called the fundamental question: why is there anything at all, rather than nothing; and how do we establish an apprehensible form for what *is*—how do we establish being? In other words, more appropriate to our immediate concern: why are the forms established by the artist of universal significance?

Form, as Heidegger has recognized, belongs to the very essence of being. Being (*Sein*) is that which achieves a limit for itself. "That which places itself in its limit, completing itself, and so stands, has form, *morphē*. Form, as the Greeks understood it, derives its essence from an emerging placing-itself-in-the-limit."[12]

Such is the form that we have seen emerging at the dawn of human history: such is the formative capacity that distinguishes *homo sapiens* from *homo faber*. For the forms of *homo faber*, the practical and functional tools of the first stages of human development, did not reach a limit of being (*Ständigkeit*), but merely expressed a restless busyness. It was not until form had reached the limit of efficiency or usefulness that it became form-in-itself, permanent being.

It then became the *logos*. According to Heidegger the basic meaning of *logos* is gathering and togetherness, and in his words, "gathering is never a mere driving together and heaping-up. It maintains in a common bond the conflicting and that which tends to part. It does not let them fall into haphazard dispersion. In thus maintaining a bond, the *logos* has the character of permeating power, of *physis*. It does not let what it holds in its power dissolve into an empty freedom from opposition, but by uniting the opposites maintains the full sharpness of their tension."[13]

Heidegger derives this meaning of *logos* from Heraclitus, and interprets one of the fragments in the Diels-Kranz arrangement (the first) as an identification of *physis* and *logos*. In what I believe to be a very faithful translation of this obscure fragment, it reads: "Although this Logos is eternally valid, yet men are unable to understand it—not only before hearing it, but even after they have heard it for the first time. That is to say, although all things come to pass in accordance with this Logos, men seem to be quite without any experience of it—at least if they are judged in the light of such words and deeds as I am here setting forth. My own method is to distinguish each thing according to its nature, and to specify how it behaves; other men, on the contrary, are as forgetful and heedless in their waking moments of what is going on around and within them as they are during sleep."[14] In another fragment (the eighth) Heraclitus says: "Opposites move back and forth, the one to the other; from out of themselves they gather themselves," or, to quote another translation: "Opposition brings concord. Out of discord comes the fairest harmony." Heidegger interprets this fragment in the sense that the conflict of opposites is a gathering, rooted in togetherness, it is *logos*. From his identification of *logos* with *physis* Heidegger passes to beauty, for what the Greeks meant by beauty was restraint. *"Art is disclosure of the being of the essent."* "The being of the essent is the supreme radiance, *i.e.,* the greatest beauty, that which is most permanent in itself . . . For us moderns, on the contrary, the beautiful is what reposes and relaxes; it is intended for enjoyment and art is a matter for pastry cooks."[15] For the Greeks beauty was the radiance of what is complete and harmonious, of what is self-contained and original. The work of art is a disclosure of being, the establishment of a pristine relation to *physis,* to the realm of things, to nature, to being itself. But, as Heidegger makes so beautifully clear, "the Greeks did not learn what *physis* is through natural phenomena, but the other way round: it was through a fundamental poetic and intellectual experience of being that they discovered what they had to call *physis*. It was this discovery that enabled them to gain a glimpse into nature in the restricted sense. Hence *physis* originally encompassed heaven as well as earth, the stone as well as the plant, the animal as well as the man, and it encompassed human history as a work of men and gods; and ultimately and first of all, it meant the gods themselves as subordinated to destiny. *Physis* means the power that emerges and the enduring realm under its sway. This power of emerging and enduring includes 'becoming' as well as 'being' in the restricted sense of inert duration. *Physis* is the process of a-rising, of emerging from the hidden, whereby the hidden is first made to stand."[16]

But what emerges is a form, *morphē*, and what emerges has form by virtue of its togetherness, its inner relatedness, its harmony. It is usually said that the Greeks had no word for art, and the word *technē* is substituted; but the Greeks had no word for art because they did not conceive it as separate from the apprehension of reality, the establishment of being, from physics and metaphysics. *Technē*, says Heidegger, was neither art nor technology, but a knowledge, the ability to plan and organize freely, to master institutions, and in justification he refers us to Plato's *Phaedrus*. "*Technē* is creating, building in the sense of a deliberate producing"; it is the ability to invent the efficient tool, but not the free form. But elsewhere Heidegger redefines *technē* as knowledge in the authentic sense, not as mere observation concerning previously unknown data, but as the actual doing which results in the production of objects,[17] "the initial and persistent looking out beyond what is given at any time." Art can then be identified with *technē* because:

[Art] is what most immediately brings being (*i.e.*, the appearing that stands there in itself) to stand, stabilizes it into something present (the work). The work of art is not primarily a work of art because it is wrought (*gewirkt*), made (we have seen that the tool satisfies these conditions), but because it brings about (*erwirkt*) being in an essent; it brings about the phenomenon in which the emerging power, *physis*, comes to shine (*scheinen*). It is through the work of art as essent being that everything else that appears and is to be found is first confirmed and made accessible, explicable, and understandable as being or not being.[18]

Art, therefore, may be regarded as "the ability, pure and simple, to accomplish, to put-into-the-work (*ins Werk setzen*), as *technē*. Such a manifesting realization of being is knowledge, and art is *technē* in this sense: as knowledge, not because it involves 'technical' skill, tools, materials."

This distinction of Heidegger's seems to be beautifully illustrated by the early evolution of artifacts as I have described it. *Technē* in the sense of skill will account for the form of the artifact as a tool designed for practical needs; but *technē* in the sense of making and manifesting brings about a form that stands there in itself, disassociated from its practical function, a configuration disclosing itself as the being of the essent.

In reading Heidegger's interpretation of the early Greek philosophy one is inevitably reminded of a philosophy that was contemporary with it, the Chinese, and there one finds an attempt to explain the establishment of being which can be closely related to early Greek thought. It is beyond my powers to attempt a correlation of the Greek and the Chinese cosmologies, but I can perhaps indicate some analogies. There is the same awareness of Being and Nonbeing, and of the mystery of the emergence of form from a primordial chaos. According to the *Huai-nan-Tzŭ*, a second century B.C. miscellaneous compilation of all schools of thought which summarizes earlier philosophic writings, two contrary principles, the *yin* and the *yang*, gradually emerged from a complex and universal energy, and by uniting with one another, these contrary principles constituted the first harmonious forms. To quote from Derk Bodde's translation of the *Huai-nan-Tzŭ:*

> When Heaven and Earth did not yet have form, there was a state of amorphous formlessness. Therefore this is termed the Great Beginning (*t'ai shih*). This Great Beginning produced an empty extensiveness, and this empty extensiveness produced the cosmos. The cosmos produced the primal fluid (*yüan ch'i*), which had its limits. That which was clear and light collected to form Heaven. That which was heavy and turbid congealed to form Earth. The union of the clear and the light was especially easy, whereas the congealing of the heavy and the turbid was particularly difficult, so that Heaven was formed first and Earth afterward.
>
> The essences of Heaven and Earth formed the *yin* and the *yang,* and the concentrated essences of the *yin* and the *yang* formed the four seasons. The scattered essences of the four seasons formed the myriad things. The hot force of *yang,* being accumulated for a long time, produced fire, and the essence of fire formed the sun. The cold force of *yin,* being accumulated for a long time, produced water, and the essence of water formed the moon. The refined essence of the excess fluid of the sun and moon formed the stars and planets. Heaven received unto itself the sun, moon, stars and planets, while Earth received water, rivers, soil and dust.[19]

This process of formation, of a gathering of opposites, a *logos,* remains on the cosmological level in Chinese thought, but the process does not end with water, rivers, soil and dust, but is extended by analogy to living plants and animals, and finally to the human race and its artifacts. The work of art is conceived as a symbol of cosmic units, as a reification of the concentrated essences of *yin* and *yang.*

A more significant analogy, perhaps, for our purpose is the evolution of the trigrams used in the process of divination as practiced in the *I Ching.* According to early Chinese historians, divination was originally made by means of the tortoise shell, which was heated with fire by the diviner, who then interpreted the cracks which appeared on its surface. The eight trigrams, and the sixty-four hexagrams derived from these by combining any two into diagrams of six lines each, were intended as a formal substitute for the chaos of lines that appeared on the heated tortoise shell, and were probably introduced at about the same time that form began to emerge as a conscious entity in the artifacts of the Chinese—the period of the Five Emperors,[20] or the Yang-Shao period as it is now usually called after the site of one of the Neolithic villages of about 3000 to 2500 B.C., discovered by Dr. J. Gunnar Andersson.[21] I am not suggesting that the parallel between the discovery of pure form in such artifacts as the axhead or the adz and the invention of the trigrams is an exact one, but we may discount the legend that the trigrams were actually invented by Fu Hsi (according to another legend he found them on the back of a dragon-horse that suddenly rose from the waters of the Yellow River). It is more probable that the legends were invented to explain the gradual evolution of formal shapes from the intricate cracks on the heated tortoise shells.

It should be observed that the form of each trigram has a sign value, or symbolic significance. The signs consist of the eight possible combinations of broken and unbroken lines in threes, and it is said that the unbroken line represents the male principle, the broken line the female principle (equally they may represent "the hot force of *yang*" and "the cold force of *yin*"). Richard Wilhelm, in his edition of the *I Ching*,[22] classifies the various attributes, images and family relationships that the eight trigrams symbolize: the details are not significant for our present purpose, but only the fact that a formal arrangement, a Gestalt, has become endowed with a sign value, or with symbolical significance. The symbols may seem fairly obvious (and should therefore more correctly be called signs)—a combination of three unbroken lines signifies the creative, the strong, heaven, and father; whereas a combination of three broken lines signifies the receptive, the yielding, earth and mother, but the symbolism becomes less obvious in the more intricate combinations, and very obscure when the eight trigrams are combined with one another to make sixty-four symbols.

Why should form have symbolic significance? —that is the question to which we must finally address ourselves, for we may assume that pure or artistic form would never have been separated from the utilitarian shape unless the mind of man had suddenly perceived a nonutilitarian significance in the shape, a manifesting realization of being. There are three possibilities:

1) That a symbolic function developed from the utilitarian function—*e.g.*, the ax used in sacrifices acquired by association a ritual significance in addition to its utilitarian purpose, and its form was on that account gradually refined.

2) That a symbolic value was attached to a form because it resembled a natural object—*e.g.*, the unbroken line is the creative male organ, the broken line the receptive female organ.

3) That the form itself became significant because it acquired harmonic proportions. We must on this supposition ask further why harmony should be significant.

I think we can dismiss the second of these possibilities for the semantic reason already given: a form that has significance because it resembles another object is not a symbol, but a sign. A symbol is only a symbol insofar as it signifies an unknown, or not otherwise expressible, perception or feeling.

We are therefore left with two values that may be symbolized in a created form: one of perception and sensation, the other of intuition and feeling. What is evident to perception and sensation is the radiance of being; what is evident to intuition and feeling is the gathering-together-in-itself, the formal restraint.

Consciousness itself is formal: not so much form-giving as form-receiving. That is to say, we understand experience insofar as it is presented to consciousness as form. "From the very first, so to speak, consciousness is a symbolizing activity. Hence one never finds in it anything barely 'given' without meaning and reference beyond itself. There is no content that is not construed according to some form."[23] That was the great affirmation that Kant made in his *Critique of Pure Reason*, and it has never been convincingly disproved. On the contrary, it has been developed in our time into an all-embracing philosophy of form by the genius of Ernst Cassirer, on whom I shall rely for my concluding observations.

There was form before there was human consciousness of form: the universe itself, the *yin* and the *yang* that emerged out of primal chaos and formed concentrated essences. Human consciousness began with the forms of perception, and human intelligence and spirituality with the representation of form. Man's freedom and his culture begins with a *will* to form. Language, the sustaining medium of his imagination, is a formal creation. Art itself is a will to form, and not merely an involuntary or instinctive reaction. "The moment of *purposiveness* is necessary for linguistic and artistic expression.

In every act of speech and in every artistic creation we find a definite teleological function."[24] Or, as Cassirer says in another place: "The artistic eye is not a passive eye that receives and registers the impression of things. It is a constructive eye, and it is only by constructive acts that we discover the beauty of natural things. The sense of beauty is the susceptibility to the dynamic life of forms, and this life cannot be apprehended except by a corresponding dynamic process in ourselves."[25]

Applying this observation to the first human artifacts that revealed artistic form, we must still ask: how did that susceptibility to the dynamic life of forms come into being?

We can only grope for an answer to this question. We know that the concept of abstract space, for example, was not discovered before the time of Democritus (460 to 360 B.C.)—it was one of the distinctive achievements of Greek thought. We cannot assume that the human beings who first discovered beauty in the Neolithic age had any abstract conceptions of space, or proportion, or harmony. Theirs was an unreflective, sensational experience. If therefore form became significant for Neolithic man, it was an act of perception and not of intelligence. Insofar as Neolithic man was purposive in giving an artistic form to his artifacts, the purpose must have been a progressive approximation toward a sense of form derived from his general experience. That is to say, man must have gradually acquired from his material environment a conditioned response to those physical properties of symmetry and harmonic proportion which his senses received from the observed form of his own body, the forms of animals and plants, the rhythm of day and night, and so on. Since form is prior to human experience, we can legitimately assume that the consciousness of form was received from the natural environment of man, and then spontaneously matched in his artifacts. But it was the form that was matched, not the appearance, and it was the form that was symbolic.

The purpose of such symbolic forms, we may assume with Heidegger and Cassirer, was to disclose meaning, to create the tools of discourse. Cassirer observes:

> Since every particular content of consciousness is situated in a network of diverse relations, by virtue of which its simple existence and self-representation contain *reference* to other and still other contents, there can and must be certain formations of consciousness in which the pure form of reference is, as it were, sensuously embodied. From this follows the characteristic two-fold nature of these formations: their bond with sensibility, which however contains within it a freedom from sensibility. In every linguistic 'sign,' in every mythical or artistic 'image,' a spiritual content, which intrinsically points beyond the whole sensory sphere, is translated into the form of the sensuous, into something visible, audible, or tangible. An independent mode of configuration appears, a specific activity of consciousness, which is differentiated from any datum of immediate sensation or perception, but makes use of these data as vehicles, as means of expression.[26]

That passage from Cassirer's great work contains, it seems to me, in concentrated essence the answer to our question. The transition from a refined but still utilitarian form, produced under necessity, is effected at the crossroads of consciousness, where forms meet and mingle; and at this encounter forms first acquire at once their freedom and their expressive function. At this moment "consciousness *creates* definite concrete sensory contents as an expression for definite complexes of meaning. And because these contents which consciousness creates are entirely in its power, it can, through them, freely 'evoke' all those meanings at any time." In other words, language and art acquire their symbolic functions: a symbolic discourse, divorced from material necessity, then becomes possible.

We cannot reconstruct or even imagine that "moment" in prehistory when form first disclosed being, when man for the first time stabilized being into the concreteness of a work of art. One might as well ask at what "moment" was consciousness born in the human race. But my object in this paper has been to show that the origins of form in art are also the origins of *logos,* of knowledge of being, of reality. Art, insofar as it has retained its primary function and not become "a matter for pastry cooks," has throughout history always been such a mode of revelation, of establishment, of naming. This was all said succinctly, in one line of verse,[27] by Hölderlin:

Was bleibet aber, stiften die Dichter.

1. Kenneth P. Oakley, *Man the Tool-Maker,* London, British Museum (1958), pp. 2–3.
2. The pioneer among chimpanzee painters was a female called Alpha, at the Yerkes Laboratory in the United States. An analytical study of her drawings was published by *The Journal of Comparative and Physiological Psychology,* vol. 44 (1951), pp. 110–111. For Dr. Morris' analysis of Congo's painting, see *The New Scientist* (August 14, 1958).
3. For a clear account of this technical development see Sir Francis H. S. Knowles, Bart., *Stone-Worker's Progress, a Study of Stone Implements in the Pitt Rivers Museum,* Oxford (1953).
4. J. Gunnar Andersson, *Children of the Yellow Earth,* London (1934), pp. 293, 318.
5. Carl Hentze, "Les jades archaïques en Chine," *Artibus Asiae* (1929), no. 4. *Cf.* also Soame Jenyns, *Chinese Archaic Jades in the British Museum,* London (1951).
6. Max Raphael, *Prehistoric Pottery and Civilization in Egypt,* New York (1947), pp. 24–25.
7. *Ibid.,* p. 25.
8. *Ibid.,* p. 55.
9. E. H. Gombrich, *Art and Illusion,* New York and London (1960).
10. Paolo Graziosi, *Palaeolithic Art,* London (1960), pp. 24–25.
11. This process of the formalization of the female figure is illustrated still more clearly in the Cycladic representations in marble of the female figure; these date from the third millennium B.C.
12. Martin Heidegger, *An Introduction to Metaphysics,* Ralph Manheim translation, New Haven (1959), p. 60.
13. *Ibid.,* p. 134.
14. Philip Wheelwright, *Heraclitus,* Princeton (1959), p. 19.
15. Heidegger, *op cit.,* p. 131.
16. *Ibid.,* pp. 14–15.
17. *Cf.* Thomas Langan, *The Meaning of Heidegger,* London (1959), p. 193.
18. *Ibid.,* p. 159. It is better to avoid, in the present discussion, the distinction between *physis* and *idea. Idea,* according to Heidegger, "is a determination of the stable insofar and only insofar as it encounters vision. But *physis* as emerging power is by the same token an appearing. Except that the appearing is ambiguous. Appearing means first: that which gathers itself, which brings-itself-to-stand in its togetherness and so stands. But second it means: that which, already standing-there, presents a front, a surface, offers an appearance to be looked at." (Heidegger, *op. cit.,* p. 180.) The Greek word for what is offered in appearance, what confronts us, is *eidos.*
19. Fung Yu-Lan, *Chinese Philosophy,* Derk Bodde translation, Peking and London (1937), vol. I, pp. 396–397.
20. Wang Pi (A.D. 226–249), the famous *I Ching* commentator, attributes their invention to the first of these mythical emperors, Fu Hsi.
21. *Cf.* Andersson, *op. cit.,* Chapters X, XII, XIII, XXI.
22. *The I Ching or Book of Changes.* The Richard Wilhelm translation rendered into English by Cary F. Baynes, 2 vols., London and New York (1951).
23. Charles W. Hendel, in the introduction to Ernst Cassirer's, *The Philosophy of Symbolic Forms,* New Haven (1953), vol. I, p. 57.
24. Ernst Cassirer, *Essay on Man,* New Haven (1944), New York (1953), p. 182.
25. *Ibid.,* p. 193.
26. Cassirer, *Philosophy of Symbolic Forms,* vol. I, p. 106.
27. "But what is lasting, the poets provide." Last line of Friedrich Hölderlin's poem "Andenken" ("Remembrance").

Judging by the traces left behind them, our earliest ancestors cherished in life and in death, above all other things: tools, containers for food, and beads. This esteem for tools and for food and its appurtenances we readily understand—but why beads?

Archaeological accounts of the earliest findings in ancient tombs record with regularity that among other artifacts buried with the dead were beads—beads of stone, shell, and clay. Remote peoples in South America, Africa, and the South Seas in the past and even today (where little remains that may be called remote) wear beads: beads of stone, shell, clay, glass, and metal. And the flourishing bead industry of the twentieth century bears tangible witness to the fact that beads are still in demand all over the world and in great quantities.

This timelessness, this universality of the appeal of beads is surely a unique and mystifying phenomenon. Even a cursory survey of the uses to which beads have lent themselves shows that they have filled a variety of needs, a surprising variety. They have served to identify their wearers, denoting status and wealth. Being small, durable, countable, and easily transportable and also so universally acceptable, they became trade goods and currency. Endowed with magic attributes, they were strung and worn next to the body which they were to protect or cure, for that magic which you have with you is the most potent.

But all of these attributes do not satisfactorily explain the lengths to which people have gone to acquire beads nor the curious attraction which they seem to have so universally exercised over men. Have they meant so many things and were they endowed with all these meanings in order to justify a more primitive and therefore more obscure fascination? Or should they simply be classified for purposes of study with the "magical potent symbols of prehistory"?

Bachofen says of the symbol, "Words confine infinity. Symbols guide the spirit, beyond the powers of the finite state of becoming, into the realm of the infinite world of existence."[1] Perhaps then we might begin our inquiry by considering the earliest known man-made sign, the first attempt to express something in form. We quote from Giedion:

> Prehistorians report that the earliest surviving man-made signs were found on a triangular grave slab discovered in the rock shelter of La Ferrassie in the Dordogne. These were small hollows in the slab, which was placed face down over a child's body. These hollows, which had no practical function, are a widespread phenomenon of paleolithic art whose symbolic significance is undefined.
>
> The magic symbols that appear most frequently and over the longest periods of prehistory are simple. They consist of fragments, the part standing for the whole: a hand, for example, represents the entire human being, and the genitalia represent fertility. But it is more difficult to give meaning to the circle. It appears in a great number of forms, large and small—as cup-shaped depressions in stone (*cupules*), colored dots and disks (*punctuations*), holes (*perforations*), often varying in shape.[2]

The circle, the disk, and the sphere, then, express something specifically and universally human —something recorded by the eye, made with the eye and the obeying hand and tool, and for the eye.

Roundness must surely be a phenomenon of the perceiving eye's experience of itself. Do we not live visually in a spherical world? No doubt this remains an unconscious component of our vision, but perhaps, for that, nonetheless dominant. With our extraordinary human eye we have the capacity to see both things close at hand and also objects and forms at great distances. When this capacity is finally fully developed we are able to see the remote stars, the waxing and waning moon, the rising and setting sun.

Awesome in their remoteness and divinely pursuing their slow progress through the spacious skies with regularity and detachment, man has everywhere reverently propitiated the sun, the moon, and the stars. They were his day and his night, his months and his years. He sought to win their benevolent attention by all the magical means he could devise. He made round forms, disks and spheres, and wore them on his person, symbols of great veneration. Are they magic microcosms of the remote light-giving forms of the macrocosm of the universe?

Among the earliest finds of amber in northern Europe and Russia are disks with a hole in the center, and this form is one of the most prevalent among the ancient burial treasures of Central America, formed there out of jade. Gold disks "like small mirrors which they wore about their necks" were the articles first noticed by Columbus' sailors on the Indians whom they encountered in the New World. American Indians of the Southwest, too, wore such disks made of bone, inlaid with bits of turquoise. The Chinese yin-yang circle which makes visual the belief in the interrelatedness and interdependence of beginning and end is another example of this form, and the list could be augmented with the description of similar forms from all over the world. In general the significance of the disk is conceded to be that it represents wholeness, completeness; it is the form of perfection.

Jade Disk, Chinese, Han Period or earlier.
Fogg Museum, Harvard University
Grenville L. Winthrop Bequest

But these are very mature and complicated ideas and, indeed, only the fully evolved eye is capable of perceiving the distant bright spheres in the heavens. Creuzer says, "In a flash the idea springs from the symbol and seizes all the senses. It is a ray direct from the depths of being and thinking, it transfixes our eyes and permeates our entire nature with an immediate perception."[3] This rings resoundingly true and forces us to seek for a more elemental source of experience in individual prehistory which has given the shining sphere its power to arouse so potent a reaction.

The study of human development has taught us to look for the nature of some of our most primitive feelings and responses in the earliest years—in the first reactions to life. Babies new to this world react to a variety of stimuli both from within and without, but the first smile of the wide-awake infant is in response to a mother's, or shall we say, a human face. Such confirmation of mutuality, of the first positive acceptance of a basic human relationship may perhaps not be evoked by the mother without quite a performance on her part of smiling, nodding, and making a variety of coaxing sounds. Yet the baby's responding smile is a triumph and is, of course, claimed by the mother as a token of her child's recognition of her presence and personality. Science, however, in its sober way, has shown us what exactly it does take to evoke a baby's smile. Psychologists first discovered that any smiling face hovering over the baby would bring forth a responding smile, that even a mask would do the same trick, and then, finally, that all that is really required is a more or less spherical bright surface with two dark, round spots painted on it or two beads attached to it in a horizontal configuration (this is mandatory) resembling eyes. The eye, then, is the first round object which drifts over the threshold of conscious perception of the human infant and to which with his first misty, unfocused gaze he finally reacts.[4] He is born ready to focus on and to react to luminous round objects. It is with the eyes that mother and child communicate before speech develops, as an adjunct to speech and whenever language fails. It is with the eyes that concern and love are communicated, and distance and anger as well. Growing maturity does not alter this eye-centeredness, for all through life our visual intercourse with others is eye-focused; the eye that blesses and curses.

When a baby is being nursed his eyes will seek the mother's. On occasion, if she turns her face away, he will cry. When several adults surround a baby his gaze will move not from person to person, but from one pair of eyes to another. A light or a pair of earrings may temporarily become the focus of his attention, but essentially it is with eyes that he seems to feel himself surrounded, eyes that he studies and with which he communicates. The face is at first perceived as only vaguely modeled—mouths make movements, but the eyes shine out with a lively reflected light.

We begin life, then, with this relatedness to eyes, and when our eyes are able to perceive both detail and distance, we still communicate with our fellow men, faster than with words and in many ways more truly, by means of our eyes. We are warmed by the friendly eye, the eye of love, chilled and frustrated by the blank look of no communication, and we long to see the eyes of one whom we fear may have grown distant or turned away from us.

The infant, however, in his small universe of home and family, learns first to fasten his hopes on the constellations of eyes which meet his, and he guides his course by their responsive signals. In later years he may focus on the distant light of the stars or on some new symbol of hope, serenity and steadfastness, and his trust in them may well prove to have been determined by the trustworthiness and constant light in the eyes which first met his in the mutuality of giving and receiving.

The loving eye, the heavenly spheres, and the man-made symbol—the disk and the bead—convey the encouraging, the reassuring look to the beholder. But the human eye is not consistently loving and benign. It manifests our worst as well as our best, malevolence as well as benediction. The malignant eye, the eye of envy and hate, has been and still is, universally feared; and religion and protective magic the world over have focused on laws, rites, incantations, and amulets to counteract its venom.

Nine of the ten commandments of the Judaeo-Christian and Moslem religions deal with transgressions so tangible that one can conceive of their implementation by lawful means in an orderly society, but the tenth, "Thou shalt not covet," forbids an inner state not open to inspection and yet leading to malignancies which men fearfully respected before religions were formulated in complicated words. When we say, "I am green with envy," we must mean that envy is a sickness of the body as well as of the spirit which we betray with unhealthy (bile green) pallor. Perhaps this is a physical admission of guilt, for later Christian teaching states unequivocally that to look is an act, an irreversible deed.

There is a malignant power, then, in the glance of hate. It is experienced as the essence of malice itself and men have justly named this phenomena the "evil eye" and have devised magic means with which to protect themselves from its attack.

Amulets, carved stones or talismans, and beads have been devised in extraordinary variety to meet man's age-old need for protection against this threat. But on these devices, painted, engraved, or incised, the most recurrent form is that of the eye itself. The evil eye, then, is to be warded off, deflected by the strength of the benign, the loving eye. No object has lent itself more readily to such protective use than the bead. That it is also decorative and has an attraction of its own only adds to its power. Indeed, a blue bead, suggesting the pure color of the sky, is itself a potent protection. To make a bead even more effective, however, it was the custom for centuries to ornament it with spots, often circumscribed by rings resembling the iris of the eye. Beads, whether circular, oval, or triangular, when so designed are known as "eye beads." Made in great quantities in earliest Egyptian times, their manufacture was continued for hundreds of years in many other parts of the world.

In Africa, eye beads are still prevalent and add a patterned and colorful note to the native necklaces. A whole necklace of eye beads, however, all "looking" in different directions, is a truly disquieting sight. The viewer's glance is first drawn to it but is soon repelled rather than charmed and shifts away for relief, proving the ornament to be an effective, and cleverly devised, defensive charm.

The ingenious idea of warding off evil with spotted eye beads is the product of the complicated human brain. Nature, however, has devised a similar kind of protection which insects and birds use quite instinctively and with proven effectiveness. Tinbergen describes the peacock butterfly which when resting on a twig resembles a dull leaf. If disturbed it instantly opens its wings disclosing four large eyes. Tests have shown that predators are in fact startled and scared away by these eyes, the scaring

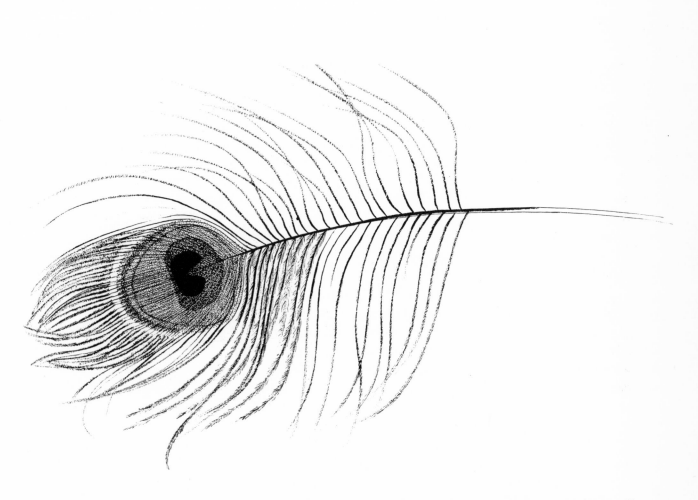

being more effective "the nearer the imitation of real eyes—that is, when they have shading, off-center 'pupils,' and even little highlights that suggest roundness." The eyed hawk moth similarly has eyes on its hind wings which are covered when protective coloring is demanded and shown when such protection fails and a second line of defense is needed.[5]

It is thought-provoking, too, that a bird, heavy in body and slow in flight, but provided with a "hundred eyes" should as a species have survived its predators. The peacock is the royal bird of the East, pacing princely gardens with majestic equanimity, the mount and companion of gods. The feathers of these colorful birds are not left to lie around in the dust, for each feathery eye provides the finder with protection. The peacock throne itself made the kings of India secure by means of its numerous jeweled eyes.

Now magic is a practical art: like produces like and similarity explains and is effect and cause. A ruby, being red, is a powerful preventative against bleeding; jaundice can be cured by the wearing of a yellow stone which extracts by attraction the unhealthy color of the skin, and with it the sickness. And nature, too, is practical. The many eyes of the peacock which are suddenly displayed when his tail is raised look out as though from a concentrated flock of big glaring birds. The eyes on the butterflies' wings are of a size appropriate to a very large animal: powerful magic indeed.

If the eye is that *ur*-form which we apprehend and take in visually with our mother's milk, we should expect to find its impress in our deepest feelings and longings and appearing in those universal manifestations of these emotions—in the symbols and forms of religion. Before gods had names known to us, before written communication of any kind, a deity existed whose worship can be traced from the earliest findings in Asia to Northern Europe. This deity, however crudely depicted as statue or graven

image, has three characteristic attributes: eyes, necklace of beads, and breasts. The staring eyes, however, are the dominant feature from which her modern name, the Eye Goddess, is derived. Her temple in Tel Brak, in the Khabur Valley in eastern Syria, has now been named the Eye Temple and dated at about 3000 B.C. The eye idols excavated there share a "rigid frontality—the same staring eyes heavily outlined with colour; even the same pattern of dots to indicate strings of beads," the eyes being "the feature of the divinity which struck the beholder most forcibly." This image with its necklace and staring eyes, considered to be indisputably connected with fertility cults, can be traced as far north as Ireland and Britain, south to Central Africa and west to the Indus Valley where the Harappa figurines also have clearly defined blobs for eyes and for their necklace beads.[6]

This ancient deity might be described as the infant's eye-view mother goddess, for her attributes are those within the infant's cognitive universe. The breasts, the nipples (the rosette is also her symbol) provide him with warm, soothing, thirst-quenching nourishment. Her eyes commune with him, they are his community. And the beads of the necklace, so we have postulated, provide a shiny multiplied stimulus which may sustain him when the mothering eye is temporarily diverted.

The heir to this ancient Eye Goddess in the Egyptian hierarchy of gods was Horus, son of Osiris. In his mythological struggle with Set, the god of storm, he lost one eye, his left eye, which was later restored. Horus is the god of the heavens and reportedly his eyes symbolize the sun and the moon. The moon waxes, wanes, and disappears and is then slowly restored, even as the fruits of the earth, even as man himself. The left eye of Horus (the feminine eye) as a symbol, then, represents the cycle of birth, death, and rebirth. But the conflict between Set and Horus was to avenge Osiris and, therefore, the lost eye was a sacrifice to Osiris. The phrase "I give to thee the eye of Horus" throughout Egyptian writings signifies the presentation of a sacrifice. In ancient Egypt the eye of Horus and the scarab (also an eye form) were the two most common symbols. "The eye of Horus acquired such a reputation that to it were ascribed peculiar strength, vigour, protective power, and safety, the rays of whose light nourished the spirits of heaven, and created things and beings."[7]

To the east in the villages of India a mother goddess was and still is worshiped, especially by the lower castes. There is considerable evidence that this mother goddess reigned supreme all over the Indian continent before the advent of the Aryans from the north with their male deities. The mother goddess, the Mata, is an all-seeing deity embracing birth and death—creation and destruction, the energy of the universe. The supreme god figure of the Brahmanical gods is Siva with his consort Pārvati and the masculine and feminine virtues are appropriately divided between them. However, Siva is endowed with a third eye, an eye in the middle of his forehead which usually remains closed. When opened under extreme provocation it flashes out death-dealing rays of destruction.

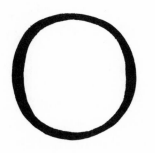

*The circle, being without
beginning or end, is a sign of God
or of Eternity. Moreover, in
contrast with the next sign, it is a
symbol of the sleeping eye of God;
"The Spirit of God moved upon
the face of the waters."*

*The open eye of God, the purpose
of Revelation;
"And God said, Let there be light."*[8]

Better known to us in the Western world are the references to the eye of God, the great Jehovah, in the book of the Bible. No graven image might be made in His likeness by the Hebrews, but their sacred writings abound with poetic expressions descriptive of His all-seeing eye. Perhaps there is some relationship between this heritage of poetic writing and the injunction against the fashioning of holy images, and for this we can be grateful since the word pictures have endured undamaged through time.

If the graphic artist is endowed with "bountiful eyes," "seeing eyes," and records the form of his vision in color, light, movement, and expression, the bard, the seer, and the poet have been artists of the word often depicted as blind, lonely, and infirm. The gift of prophecy, it is said, may be bought only at the price of the right eye, for one eye of him who sees the past and the future must be turned inward in reflection.

Herbert Read speaks of the eye of infancy and of childhood as the "innocent eye." This is surely the eye that perceives out of the pure pleasure of exercising its natural function with, as he says, "a virgin sensibility." Some of this quality may be preserved in maturity and is essential in the artist; but how is it lost? What is the guilty eye? The poet who composed the third chapter of Genesis, in describing the temptation and fall of Adam and Eve, puts the following words into the mouth of the "subtil" snake as he tempts with the forbidden fruit. "For God doth know that in the day ye eat thereof, then *your eyes shall be opened,* and ye shall be as gods, knowing good and evil. And when Eve *saw* that the tree was good for food, and that it was *pleasant to the eyes,* and a tree to be desired to make one wise she did eat the fruit and shared it with Adam. And the *eyes of them both were opened,* and they knew that they naked." And they covered themselves with fig leaves and hid for shame.

So, it would seem, the price of wisdom, of the knowledge of good and evil, is the loss of the innocent eye. Looking is no longer enough in itself. Looking becomes a means to an end, a tool—we lose paradise and are left with a deep and abiding nostalgia. But the prophets exhort the Edenless descendants of Adam and Eve and hold out hope and comfort, for "he whose eye is open" and obeys the law will see that "the commandment of the Lord is pure, enlightening the eyes." For those that turn away from His holy ways there is threat. "When ye spread forth your hands I will hide mine eyes from you," but for those that lead a godly life there is promise, "For I will set mine eyes upon them for good."

58

The Bible abounds in imagery concerning the eye of God which is upon His people and "runs to and fro throughout the whole earth" giving light and gracious blessing. In the Byzantine Christian churches, perhaps as a heritage from Asia Minor, the eye of God is again depicted in graphic form looking down from wall or ceiling and with pervading glance encompassing and penetrating the innermost thoughts and feelings of the assembled congregation. Among the manifestations of Western religious symbolism, too, we should not overlook the ring, the crown, and the halo.

The bead has led us to the disk and the sphere, symbols which "encompass the whole in an instant." The symbol has led us to its possible archetype, its *ur*-form, the eye.

Might one not then speculate that the eye, the eye itself as an object, is the *ur*-phenomenon of aesthetic visual delight? In his book, *The Innocent Eye*, Herbert Read writes:

> The echoes of my life which I find in my early childhood are too many to be dismissed as vain coincidences; but it is perhaps my conscious life which is the echo, the only real experiences in life being those lived with a virgin sensibility—*so that we only hear a tone once, only see a colour once, see, hear, touch, taste and smell everything but once, the first time.* All life is an echo of our first sensations, and we build up our consciousness, our whole mental life, by variations and combinations of these elementary sensations. But it is more complicated than that, for the senses apprehend not only colours and tones and shapes, but also patterns and atmospheres, and our first discovery of these determines the larger patterns and subtler atmospheres of all our subsequent existence.[9]

Once, then, we experienced wholeness, once we perceived form, movement, color, light, and expression in one completely satisfying form. Let us consider how essential elements of the whole experience draw on some early source of conscious and unconscious memory.

The eye is, so we have been asserting, the most honest agent of *communication*. Is it not, perhaps, the deep well at the bottom of which truth is said to be found? And the *form* of the eye may indeed be the archetype of that most ancient symbol, the sphere.

Moreover, our language is rich in expressions which describe the *movement* of the eye. Eyes, we say, open, widen, narrow, and close. They catch, cast, draw, repel, and blink; they dance and wink, fix and freeze, soften, melt, wander, and exult. The black pupil of the eye actually expands and contracts, adding involuntary action to the almost constant action of the eyeball and eyelid. We both see this movement and simultaneously experience it as a function of our own eyes, thereby compounding its impact on our awareness. For the infant, visually absorbed in his mother's eyes, a lively world of movement is early discernible.

Light is the attribute most evocative of the eye. It receives and gives forth light, it glistens, gleams, shines, glitters, and glares. All variations and quantities of light glow in the eye and are reflected in it. When it is dulled and misted over, life itself loses its luster. Light then, its focus, its variety, its play, lives in the eye and enchants the beholder.

Blue, gray, green, golden brown, dark brown are the *colors* of the iris of the eye and all of these may be flecked, varied, and iridescent as the word "iris" suggests. Horus' left eye was represented with green (malachite) as it waxed and was restored, with red (carnelian) as wounded it waned and disappeared. In the eye we associate illness, wound, or extreme anger with red. But all the other colors of the rainbow are there and, indeed, the goddess Iris is the goddess of the rainbow.

In the youthful eye the colorful iris is set off by the bluish-white of the eyeball and darkens into the shaded, fringed area surrounding the black pupil. The aging iris loses the brilliance of its color and its clear, spherical outline and the eyeball becomes yellowish and red-veined. Agee's account of looking, as a child, into his aged great-grandmother's eyes is haunting.

> They were just color: seen close as this, there was color through a dot at the middle, dim as blue-black oil, and then a circle of blue so pale it was almost white, that looked like glass, smashed into a thousand dimly sparkling pieces, smashed and infinitely old and patient, and then a ring of dark blue, so fine and sharp no needle could have drawn it, and then a clotted yellow full of tiny squiggles of blood, and then a wrong-side furl of red-bronze, and little black lashes. Vague light sparkled in the crackled blue of the eye like some kind of remote ancestor's anger, and the sadness of time dwelt in the blue-breathing, oily center, lost and alone and far away, deeper than the deepest well.[10]

The "raison d'être of the symbol," writes Creuzer, "lies in the human urge to express that which is inherently inexpressible."[11] This human urge may well be that impelling force which sponsors all creative endeavor; the endeavor to effect a restitution of a positive and affirming experience of order in a new form and on a higher level.

Assuming, then, the validity of the hypothesis that the early experience of the eye as a visual object remains a fundamental configuration, let us listen to the words used by artists in describing their relationship to the process of painting itself.

> Painting thus becomes an act of adoration, an avowal of faith in the validity of existence. (Jean Hélion)[12]

> Therefore I would say that a subject painted by myself is simply a modification of pre-existing pictorial relationships. (Juan Gris)[13]

> This is a kind of secret language composed of magic runes, that exists before words, and springs from that era when what men imagined and divined was far more real and true than what they saw—when that was the sole reality. (Joan Miró)[14]

> Am I fooling myself? is the impression my picture gives me of containing *reality* within it (as if by some magic I had evoked a warmth, a throbbing, a breathing, so compelling as to strike fear, as if I had hit on a dangerous mechanism for creating life, without knowing how or when), is this impression true only for me, or is it equally so for everyone who looks at the picture? . . . All the better if the literal intention of the picture is now in suspense: from this moment on an intense *reality* suffuses it, now it becomes a highly potent means of evoking and relating all sorts of ideas, a means of conveying an awareness of kinships, resemblances, identifications—a means of meditation. (Jean Dubuffet)[15]

A painter stretches his canvas over a square or rectangular form. This is convenient because fabric, having been so woven, lends itself to being held firmly, with tension, in this manner. The finished painting is then framed and hung in a free space on the wall of a room, thus breaking up that space, adding a new dimension, a look beyond the wall or through it—in short, a window. Our windows are now rectangular or square—but this was not always so. In earlier times they were small and arched or round, a form we retain for the portholes of ships. They were called in Old English *windauga*, wind-eye, the eyes of the house through which one looked out at the world, and through which the world looked in.

The fine painting that we study intensively and study repeatedly until we *see* it, moves us. It heightens our awareness and may lift our spirits or release our tears. But in either case it restores order in our inner world and gives form to the feeling it evokes. It communicates with us adding new dimensions, a universality, to our response. We contemplate it with deep appreciation and love and the painting returns our gaze, restoring, nourishing, and reaffirming our relationship with the human condition. Solemnly or gaily it says, "yes." We learned this exchange in the very beginnings of our existence.

". . . memory is a flower which only opens fully in the kingdom of Heaven, where the eye is eternally innocent." (Herbert Read)

1. Johann Jakob Bachofen, *Versuch über die Gräber Symbolik der Alten,* quoted by S. Giedion, "The Roots of Symbolic Expression," in *Daedalus,* vol. 89, no. 1 (Winter, 1960), p. 30.
2. Giedion, *op. cit.,* pp. 26–27.
3. Friedrich Creuzer, *Symbolik und Mythologie der Alten Völker, besonders der Griechen,* quoted by Giedion, *op. cit.,* p. 31.
4. Peter H. Wolff, "Observations on the Early Development of Smiling," *Determinants of Infant Behavior; Proceedings, Tavistock Study Group on Mother-Infant Interaction,* London (1959); and René A. Spitz, "The Smiling Response: A Contribution to the Ontogenesis of Social Relations," *Genetic Psychology Monographs,* vol. 34, 1st section (August, 1946), Worcester, Mass., Clark University.
5. Nikolaas Tinbergen, "The Butterfly's Evil Eye," in *Animals* (1964), p. 214.
6. Osbert G. S. Crawford, *The Eye Goddess,* London (1957).
7. Samuel A. Mercer, *Horus, Royal God of Egypt,* Grafton, Mass., Society of Oriental Research (1942).
8. Rudolf Koch, *The Book of Signs* (trans. from the German by Vyvyan Holland), New York, Dover Publications (1930).
9. Herbert Read, *The Innocent Eye,* London, Faber and Faber (1933) and New York, H. Holt & Co. (1947).
10. James Agee, *A Death in the Family,* New York, McDowell, Obolensky, Inc. (1957), p. 239.
11. Friedrich Creuzer, quoted by Giedion, *op. cit.,* p. 32.
12. "Statements and Documents; Artists on Art and Reality, on Their Work, and on Values," *Daedalus* (Winter, 1960), p. 100.
13. Daniel Henry Kahnweiler, *Juan Gris: His Life and Work* (trans. from the French by Douglas Cooper), London, Lund, Humphries (1947), pp. 138–139. Quoted also in *Daedalus* (Winter, 1960), p. 83.
14. *XXè Siècle,* Giorgio di San Lazzaro, editor, no. 9 (June, 1957); quoted also in *Daedalus* (Winter, 1960), p. 93.
15. *XXè Siècle . . . ;* quoted also in *Daedalus* (Winter, 1960), pp. 95–96.

KAZUHIKO EGAWA

THE FUNDAMENTAL ELEMENTS OF JAPANESE OBJECT-MAKING

Visitors to Japan arriving at Tokyo by air at night often express their great wonderment at the sight of the mammoth city spread below, ablaze with countless spectacular neon-lit advertisements. Indeed, the amazing transformation Japan has undergone in recent years is symbolized in her neon advertisements, elevated highways, and ultramodern office buildings. Signs of the rapid growth of science and technology in Japan can be noted also in such high-efficiency products as electron microscopes, cameras, and transistor radios which she manufactures and exports to the world. Modernization has certainly made the life of the Japanese people more affluent, more comfortable, and less bound to drudgery. This is the reason why the Japanese have been so eager to foster it.

In the midst of this frenzied modernization, however, it is almost impossible to keep track of the old tradition in Japanese object-making, unless one witness some religious ceremonies or customs surviving in remote provincial towns. Is it then possible that modern civilization and technology can completely destroy traditional culture? This is a question which does not pose itself uniquely in the case of modern Japan, but indeed is a problem faced by all the civilized nations of the world. On profound examination, however, it is seen that traditions cannot so easily perish. This is probably because men's lives are so deeply rooted in external physical conditions: tradition will survive unless climate, physical environment, and the people drastically change.

Much of tradition does seem to have vanished from sight in Japan, but there still remains something, beyond mere objects and forms, that is too durable to have been extinguished. That is the sincerity, the ingenuousness, and the industry of Japanese object-makers. These are qualities born of a long tradition. John Dewey rightly observed, "There is no art in which there is only a single tradition." Object-making, like any other human creative activity, is founded on much more than a mere technical tradition. Nothing is born of object-making—be it fine art or applied art or folk art—when necessity and inevitability are lacking. As in the working of nature, human energies are expended only when there is necessity. Forms are thus created inevitably out of object-making, and the climate, the physical environment, and the temper of the people determine the course of their development. Forms born of necessity

will inevitably be simple and functional. The more functional they are, the more imbued are they with profound significance. As this significance deepens so does the spirituality of the forms.

Simplicity, functionality, and spiritualization are the fundamental elements of Japanese object-making. These qualities can be recognized already in the relics of prehistoric Japan. Indeed, the essential roots of Japanese art are found in these objects of the remote past, and the modern Japanese cannot fail to identify their sensibility with that which they recognize in them. Technical tradition may certainly have vanished from the surface of Japanese life, but tradition in the sense of these fundamental aesthetic elements still survives in the creative activities of modern Japan.

When we examine the stone artifacts made at the dawn of human civilization we understand that object-making by mankind indeed began with the striving for simplicity, functionality, and spiritualization. These qualities are very evident in the stone artifacts and pottery of the Stone Age culture of Japan. Influenced by the climate, the environment, and the manner of living of the people, the ideals embodied in these prehistoric works became a tradition of Japanese craftsmen.

Figs. 1–4. Examples of Jomon ware, the Stone Age pottery of Japan. Photos Yompachi Fujimoto.

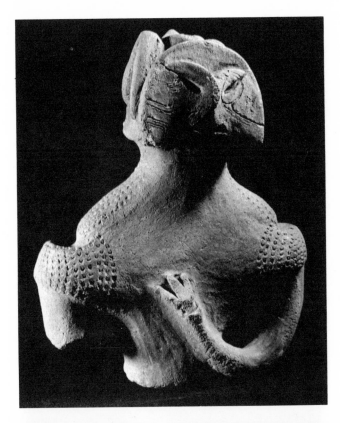

Figs. 5–7. Joman pottery figurines of ancient Japan. Photos Yompachi Fujimoto.

The Stone Age pottery of Japan has been given the name of Jomon ware, or "rope-pattern" ware, because their simple surfaces are decorated with pressed rope patterns. These earliest examples of Japanese object-making come from a period when the people were engaged in hunting and fishing for a livelihood. This period spans a long space of time, from about 7500 to roughly 300 B.C. Here, in the incipient stages of the man-made object in Japan, can already be seen an attitude of sincerity and willingness to respond to necessity. True, elaborate examples, where shapes are purposely varied and decorative effects sought, can be found in the later Jomon ware, but although elaborate in surface decorations, the method of manufacture is essentially simple, straightforward, and free of inner conflict. In this can be seen a deeply rooted sensibility which was later to govern as a tradition all Japanese object-making. Throughout the history of Japanese crafts this sensibility can be perceived not only visually in forms, but also intuitively through forms.

In the objects of the succeeding epoch, known as the Yayoi period, there is discernible not only a greater refinement in the simplicity and function of form, but a much greater spiritualization of forms as religion came to play an increasingly important role in Japanese society. The Yayoi period covers about six hundred years from 300 B.C. to approximately A.D. 300. In contrast to the Jomon period the culture of the Yayoi was based on agriculture. This period is well known for its pottery, the simple *sueki*-type ware and *haniwa* or clay figures. *Haniwa* were developed from hollow, cylindrical pottery posts, implanted in the ground along the exterior of tombs of high-ranking personages to prevent the erosion of the earth. These simple but expressive images of warriors and ladies, birds, monkeys and horses, or models of houses and ships, indicate not only a considerably high level of formal attainment, but also a deepening of the spiritual life of the people.

Figs. 8–10. *Haniwa* figures of the Yayoi period.
Photos Yompachi Fujimoto.

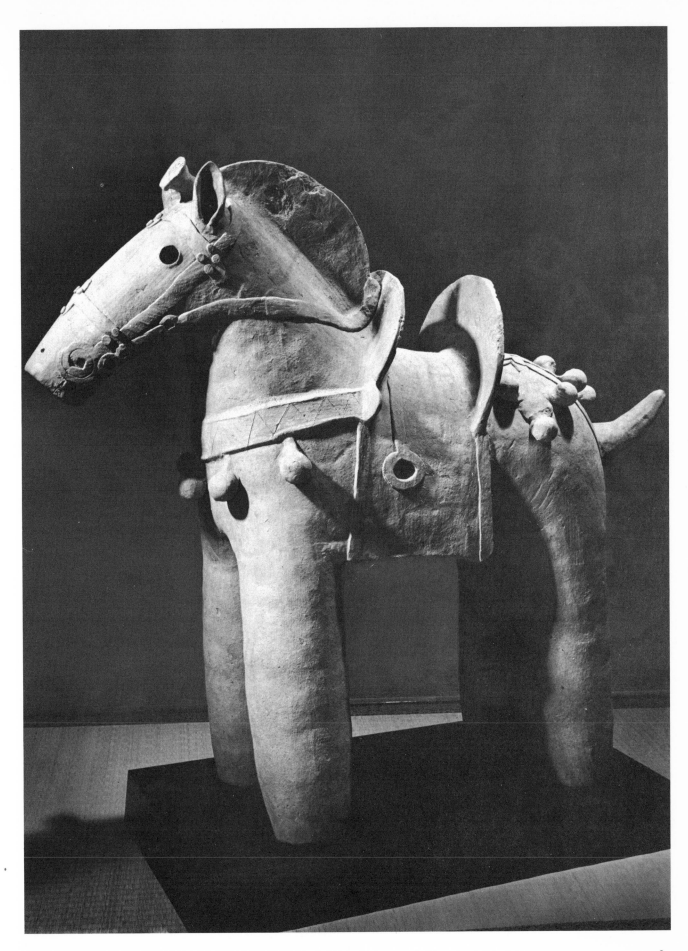

Fig. 11. *Haniwa* model of a dwelling house of the Yayoi period. Photo Yompachi Fujimoto.

Fig. 12. Ise Shrine: its architectural form dates back to the third century. Photo Yoshio Watanabe.

Shown here is a *haniwa* which represents a dwelling house of the time, probably the manor of a local lord. This clay model bears a strong resemblance to the architecture of the Ise Shrine, which retains the ancient style. Built of plain, unwashed wood, the architecture of the shrine shows the simplicity, naïveté and neatness of design befitting the sanctuary which is dedicated to the ancestoral deities of the imperial family. The beauty of this shrine has been looked upon as the symbol of Japanese architectural aesthetics. The sensibility embodied in the shrine building has been a source of inspiration to craftsmen throughout the history of Japanese object-making.

The Izumo Shrine, still earlier than the Ise Shrine, has been another source of inspiration to the Japanese ideals of beauty. This shrine is dedicated to a different lineage of ancient deities, and in contrast to the Ise Shrine which is closed, or exclusive, the precinct and architecture of the Izumo Shrine are more open, or inclusive. Yet here again, the same fundamental aesthetic ideals can be seen to have guided its creation.

Fig. 13. Izumo Shrine: its architectural form is believed to date back to the first century.

13

The course of the history of object-making in Japan was drastically altered when the Buddhism of the Asiatic mainland made its way via Korea to Japan, flooding the country with its accompanying arts. In point of fact, the advanced technique of the mainland had been seeping into the country well before this era known as the period of the Ancient Burial Mounds. The Japanese had always welcomed whatever came from a civilization more advanced than theirs. The position of the Japanese Islands, separated by only narrow straits from the Asiatic mainland, had made the people extremely comprehensive and adept at assimilating foreign elements into their culture. But what is noteworthy is the fact that these foreign elements have always been digested and adapted to the native ideals of beauty.

In the subsequent Asuka (552–645), Nara (646–793) and Fujiwara (901–1183) periods numerous Buddhist temples were erected, and an enormous amount of Buddhist sculpture produced, not only by Japanese but also by Chinese and Korean architects and sculptors. As these foreign artists fused with the native talent, alien styles of architecture and sculpture merged into Japanese tradition.

One sees this fusion of styles in the temple architecture of the Asuka, Nara, and Fujiwara periods, especially in the pagodas—beautiful pagodas of the Horyu-ji, the Yakushi-ji, the Muro-ji, and the Daigo-ji, to cite a few. These were the periods in which Japanese culture blossomed forth at the inspiration of Buddhism, and all these examples can really be said to be native in their methods of construction and style. The Byodo-in Temple in Uji near Kyoto, which was built a little later than these other temples, is the most representative of native Buddhist architecture.

14

70

15

In the Kamakura period (1186–1333) the warriors rose to power, ruled, and contended with one another for supremacy. In the latter half of the fourteenth century Shogun Ashikaga-Yoshimitsu erected the Kinkaku-ji, or Golden Pavilion, in Kyoto. In the fifteenth century the Noh, the Tea Ceremony, and the Flower Arrangement were widely practiced—an indication that sensibilities purely native had become an active creative force.

Peace was restored in the Edo period (1615–1866), which was an era of feudal lords and the newly risen merchant class, the *chonin*. In the ancient capital of Kyoto, the arts enjoyed the patronage of both the court aristocracy and the townspeople. The Katsura Imperial Palace in the suburbs of Kyoto came into existence under just such favorable circumstances in the early seventeenth century. It was built for Prince Toshihito, and later additions were made by his son Toshitada.

The unsurpassed beauty of the palace buildings and gardens has been the object of praise of many visiting foreign specialists, among whom may be mentioned Bruno Taut, Walter Gropius, and Le Corbusier. The Katsura Palace is the epitome of Japanese aesthetic ideals. Its buildings and landscaped gardens are the embodiment of the traditional elements of Japanese object-making: simplicity, functionality, and spiritualization. These fundamental principles can be seen in the stone-paved paths leading to and from the main buildings, in the varying shapes and sizes of their stones, and in the bold patterns into which they are masterfully combined. The same ideals can be seen in the arrangement of rooms, in the windows with elegant, translucent, white paper sliding screens, in the latticework of the transom windows, in the design of *tokonoma*, or alcoves, in the stone bridges spanning the pond, in the small stone lanterns perched by the inlets or half-hidden behind a tree. All these are simple and pure in design and imbued with life, merging so harmoniously with surrounding nature.

We cannot overlook the important role played by the Tea Ceremony, which may be regarded as another form of Japanese creation embodying the traditional aesthetic. The buildings and gardens of the Katsura Palace cannot be fully appreciated without a knowledge of the spirit of the Tea Ceremony. Indeed, the whole palace and its several tea arbors are designed in accordance with the aesthetic ideals of the Tea.

Figs. 16–20. Views of the buildings and gardens of the Katsura Palace, near Kyoto, early seventeenth century. Photos Yasuhiro Ishimoto.

21

22

Turning our eyes once again to present-day Japan, we see that modernization spurred by the advances of science and technology is rapidly changing the environment and the mode of living of the Japanese people. Modernization is not confined to city areas; it is altering the entire face of the nation, and seems to be changing the very roots of Japanese civilization. The great progress in transportation, communication, and international trade is every day making the globe smaller and civilizations uniform, so that man-made objects of one nation look almost identical with those of another. To all appearances, local artistic tradition is dying. But, as I have said at the beginning of this paper, on close examination one finds that the indigenous tradition built up over many centuries will not so easily be extinguished. Indeed, keen eyes will recognize in the works of the new generation of artists those traditional ideals of Japanese object-making: simplicity, functionality, and spiritualization. The fact that we find traditional aesthetic sensibilities surviving in architecture, in industrial design, and in all types of forms created in our modern Japan—no matter how new the material, method, or style—is proof of the enduring strength of the Japanese aesthetic ideals. In the foregoing, I have attempted a very rough survey of the role which the three traditional ideals of beauty have played in the history of object-making in Japan, from ancient to modern times, by referring to a few among many examples. These examples are numberless today as they have been in the past.

Fig. 21. Pottery lantern for lobby or garden by contemporary craft designer, Mosuke Yoshitake.

Fig. 22. Suspended sculpture by Michio Ihara for a modern office building in Tokyo.

Fig. 23. Contemporary Buddhist *Tengai* or baldachin in the Josen-ji, temple of the Nichren sect, Tokyo.

Fig. 24. Sliding doors designed by Kiyoshi Awazu for the newly built office of the Izumo Shrine. Photo Masao Arai.

23

24

MICHAEL J. BLEE

THE MEETING: MAN AND MAN-MADE OBJECT
ARCHITECTURAL IMPLICATIONS

The contemporary architect, in common with all those whose concern is with problems of form, is most painfully aware that there is no longer a single architectural construct for man's image of his world, no single embodiment of his relationship with the world. The confined and defined local statement which comprised a regional or geographic tradition is no longer possible or valid in a world where communication physically and intellectually has made an anachronism of the closed society. In the inevitable ambivalence that results there can be no consistency or maintenance of direction; the scale and intensity of the bombardment of influences which is characteristic of an open society must continually deny that reasonably static condition from which a reasoned statement—a tradition —can emerge.

For the majority of architects the problem is never stated in these terms; preoccupation with new materials, techniques, planning problems, etc., tends to obscure or crowd out such considerations. Else recourse to such thinking is regarded as appropriate in the region of pure theory from which only the unrealistic or utopian conclusion remote from live and pressing problems can emerge. Nevertheless, it is realized that the work of those few who are guided by a particular estimate of man and his relationship with his world—both natural and man-made—and who seek a construct for this image, is marked by that lack of superficial form-gimmicks which is typical of all true and total architecture. The work of such "masters" may provoke one of two reactions: either copying without understanding and therefore a misapplication of the forms which embody their individual estimate of man and his relationship with the world; or an attempt to discover the nature and quality of this equation in order to arrive at an equivalent conviction. The former represents the familiar methods of architectural plagiarism, of fashion, stylism, etc.; the latter the more difficult path of seeking a design philosophy embodying a coherent personal estimate of the right relationship between man and his world.

In the context of this present volume the pursuit of such fundamentals is in order. It is my purpose here simply to trace an individual probe with specifically architectural implications, seeking to reveal the kind of problems with which the architect of today is concerned, particularly in terms of the equation: man—man-made object. This will amount to nothing more than the suggestion of a climate of thought and feeling within which the creation of a contemporary environment might occur. For it is important to the architect that such theory lead to a creative conclusion, and above all a conclusion that is socially as well as individually valid. (Certain modern masters have created environments which are consistent and balanced but of a predominantly personal validity. The kind of relationship which they establish errs in the direction of excessive clarity and restriction; but this remains a rare and necessary counter to the predominant condition of uncertainty.) It is not my purpose here to indicate the translation of idea into form, but to imply the quality of awareness necessary; not to outline a comprehensive philosophy built from a tangle of personal theories and definitions, but rather to suggest an individual "habitus"[1] that will suffuse thought and creative art.

The individual or collective involvement in such thinking must be motivated by the need to discover certain lines of shaping that are dedicated to this particular end—namely, of articulating, embodying, perfecting a particular man-world relationship; this while accepting materialism and the machine, accepting also tradition and craft, primordial images and chthonic powers, and not by re-

treating to a snug and defined domain of craft or of technology. Ideally, the success of such probing will be the suggestion of a formative discipline that will shape all decisions and acts, replacing the diverse and superficial pressures of style, individualism, fashion.

This then is no more than a particular approach to the predicament shared by artist and architect alike. An approach which seeks simply a general attitude, an awareness that will have positive creative implications, by focusing on the relationship between man and man-made object. This in the belief that the ambivalence which is characteristic of the present predicament may be approached most effectively through a study of this relationship.

It is only as a necessary platform for this discussion that the need for examining the nature of this predicament arises. Its formal manifestations are all too obvious, it is more difficult to pinpoint the exact cause—a host of arguments appear equally tenable depending on the method of approach and the point to be proved. In terms of this study it may be categorically defined as the failure to achieve a coherent, articulate, and systematic relationship between man and his world, particularly in the profusion of man-made objects. And as a natural corollary to this; the inability to make coherent and consistent value judgments, to determine what should be the basis of such judgments and the criteria of their correctness.

In the face of this predicament a multiplicity of often irrelevant criteria have emerged which serve to select and discriminate, to give some shape and apparent meaning to the relationships with a profusion of man-made objects; a profusion contributed not only by the machine, but by the new extension in space and time to other countries and cultures. Such means of selective judgment may be based on a rigid aesthetic, a particular fashion, a particular vision or creed; a humanist taste, a romantic vision, a sales-provoked attitude.

These criteria are accompanied by certain fixed attitudes that predetermine the relationships possible between man and man-made object. Of these the most obvious and prevalent today is that of materialism. The possessive relationship, where the criteria of judgment are based on ideas consciously or unconsciously held of status, value, etc. Alongside this exist the less suspect but equally inhibiting attitudes of the humanist seeking to impose fixed and exclusive formal criteria, and the romantic laying stress on the associational and the sensual.

Whatever the position—intellectual, statistical, functional—each provides its limiting and comfortable focus, denying whole groups of man-made objects, condemning whole areas of relationship. To the "humanist" the peasant hut and craft product, the fetish or totem, represent simply earlier stages in object-shaping, a savage man-world relationship which civilized man has left far behind. To the "romantic" the "machine for living," the machine-made product, represent a denial of the spiritual without which the relationship between man and object is meaningless. To the sales-oriented materialist that which is not fashionable or expressive of status is "square." But neither the focus on the man-made object, its formal attributes, its style, nor on the attitudes of man which dictate the nature of his response, can provide the kind of comprehensive solution to the predicament which is so sorely needed. For both specific object and specific attitude are bound to be limiting, whereas the world today is characterized by a breakdown of all space-time barriers. The creation of confined territories to be ardently defended is a dangerous occupation, aesthetically as well as politically. In more specific terms, the architect today is quite as likely to be exposed to Japanese, Aztec, or Indian architecture, as to that of Renaissance Italy or contemporary Brazil. Fixed and conveniently limiting attitudes or formal criteria are equally incapable of embracing such diverse areas, of allowing that total relationship which is creative rather than derivative. Equally suspect is that attitude of nebulous and unquestioning catholicism, that replaces a taste which may be limited but is at least discriminating, and that regards any object touched or shaped by man as meaningful.

These then are the kind of problems which go to make up the contemporary predicament insofar as it may be discovered in a confused relationship between man and man-made object. They give cause for violent partisan argument, they condemn, prescribe, dictate, exclude with assumed authority. There is often little or no communion between opposing positions and life itself is thereby deformed, unbalanced, and partial.

The thought and work of certain contemporary architects suggests that this confusion—and the consequent absence of an agreed construct—may be resolved if the focus of attention is shifted to the area between man and man-made object. It is the nature of the equation, its form and not the factors, which then becomes most important. Stated in slightly different terms, attention focuses on the quality of experience rather than the form which evokes it or the attitude which encourages it; judgment is then concerned with the quality of this experience; value inheres in the relationship between rather than in the observer attitude or object form.[2] This shift does not deny the existence of the man-made object or the significance of the observer attitude—this would obviously be absurd—but it does affirm as of positive significance the taut "negative" area between.

At this stage we are not concerned with the creative implications of this position, simply with discovering the attitude to the man-made object that is implicit in its acceptance. Those who maintain partisan positions—whether based upon specific form systems or specific observer positions—must ever remain in opposing camps, unwilling to concede to each other or to this shift in emphasis which so effectively undermines their respective domains. The classicist must see this shift as a denial of discipline, a denial of absolute values that are regarded as sacrosanct; the romantic as a failure to dis-

criminate between feeling and form. The concentration on the interval between—on the experience which is a live relationship—must acknowledge a certain truth in both positions, finding them in no way incompatible. For there are formal and informal relationships which may prove equally real and vital as experience. The moment of meeting is no longer clouded by inhibiting preconceptions, it is no longer measured against a fixed expectation. Other considerations become of greater importance. It is necessary then to consider the actual conditions of relating as more important than forms or attitudes. The climate of an effective relationship, the "mechanics" of relating, are then the center of focus. It is for this reason that a closer understanding of man becomes essential; there is a need to appreciate his function as an ecological unit and to appreciate the nature of his psychosomatic responses to shaped environment, to the man-made object both individually and collectively.[3] The architect in particular discovers the pressing need to extend his knowledge into unfamiliar disciplines, disciplines at present ill-equipped to furnish him with information of creative value.

The motivation for the extension of the architect's area of concern must be simply the desire to arrive at clear-cut conclusions on individual and collective modes of relating, in order that his work may take these as formative, and so that he may be able to make full creative use of his own experiences. Such foci may have characteristics that bear no relationship to classic or romantic precepts, and have neither geometric nor organic form equivalents. But unless they are clearly established, the shift must fail to achieve consistency and structure, and substitute vagueness for a limited but comparative precision.

Fundamental requirements of a successful and meaningful relationship (requirements that may frequently be deduced by common sense and without resort to specialist study), are often ignored when the focus is objective and formal; pretentious patterns are imposed with total disregard for their results at the level of experience. But the concern for relationships, the interest in the new biology and the social sciences that grows from experiential concern, does not deny the need for formal techniques necessary to shape and control relationships. Indeed, such denial is necessary only if specific forms rather than specific relationships are insisted upon. It would not be necessary to deny a formal solution on the grounds of failure to satisfy certain biological or sociological requirements, but rather on the basis of a breakdown in relationship under ineffectual conditions of "meeting."

And in reverse, the criticism of a biological or sociological solution on the grounds of incoherency or lack of order is equally irrelevant. Rather it is the failure to articulate a relationship, to clarify an experience, that should be condemned. If the relationship is real and meaningful, then the means to achieve that experience are fully justified whether formal or informal, organic or geometric. The shift is not to an exclusive position but to an inclusive vision. Nothing is denied; particular modes of shaping are subsumed within the primary concern that the correct relationship should be provoked. It is this primary concern that determines subsequent shaping, providing only that it is directional and selective.

The detailed study of conditions of relating is the province of sociological disciplines, but the kinds of condition that are essential to a meaningful relationship are largely self-evident. To suggest them is not to impose some new formula to which formal discipline must be subservient. For this is no new situation requiring scientific confirmation, indeed, all great architecture has satisfied these conditions to the full; though the art historian has often paid little attention to them, they have always existed at the moment when direct experience has provoked wonder, a life-enhancing intuition of the infinite.

Perhaps the most necessary and elemental condition of effective relationship is that of identity. (The discussion here, in such loose terms of precisely definable psychological concepts, is intended only as an indication of those concerns that rightly fall within the field of this new focus, directly relevant to the creative process.) The identity may occur at many levels from the physical to the spiritual, and in different modes from the individual to the collective. Without this initial sympathy no active relationship can exist, no experience can achieve life. At the individual and esoteric level such identity may exist between the Indian beggar and his patch of swept earth between temple buttresses, where pin-ups and graffito doodles proclaim possession of place and establish ownership of object. In this case the situation is unique and the relationship cannot be shared, but in a very real sense there exist here conditions satisfying a basic definition of architecture as a meaningful relationship between man and his particular shaped place. It is from this seminal condition that relationship grows to that spiritual and collective identity which is great architecture, to the life-enhancing experience of the cathedral or temple. The encouragement of such identity has been the direct function of all anthropomorphic systems of architecture, particularly that of the Classical orders, but equally in the hierarchy of identity found in the mounting scale of wall aediculae to nave tracery in the Gothic cathedral.[4] Patterns of collective identity have not always been as systematic or as conscious, however; an intuitive empathy between society and environment created the balanced pattern of identity that is discovered in the Italian hill-town or the Byzantine monastery. The complex conditions of contemporary society and the absence of a consistent basis for identity makes reliance on intuition unrealistic, and resort to a single anthropomorphic formula inhibiting. The knowledge that social science and psychology can contribute to this problem of identity in contemporary society is therefore of extreme importance and helps toward a degree of conscious exactitude, at present lacking.

Tradition and memory represent the projection of identity into the time dimension, introducing another condition of effective relationship, that of association. The moment of active relationship has direct meaning only insofar as it both relates the experience to some known patterning or

some previous encounter (even if but intuitively or unconsciously registered) and at the same time extends and enlarges experience. Without association—the organic growth of interrelationships in space and time—the experience must remain dry and sterile, and there can be little or no communication. Again tradition, unconsciously accepted as an integral part of a folk society or an established culture, guarantees this association requirement. The contemporary denial of tradition, the insistence on the new and the transient suggests that the familiar is without value. Yet the advertiser's search to establish the "brand image" reflects this need to establish an association pattern, to identify. For without some kind of association there is no common ground between successive experiences and therefore no chance of communication. It is this communication—involving the reciprocal interaction of man and object—that is essential to effective relationship, for without effective communication during an experience there can be no sense and the experience must remain meaningless. This predicament is only too common today. Town-planners concerned with the perceptual image of the city, designers who discuss association and identity patterns, are attempting to tackle these problems by a direct attack on experience.[5] It remains for the creative architect to embody conclusions arrived at with the help of other disciplines. Focus on the relationship between will alone ensure balance.

But neither the shift in focus nor the total reliance on findings of sociologists and psychologists can ensure consistency. This must depend wholly on the individual, whether creator or perceiver. It is not sufficient to maintain that he must acquire further knowledge about human behavior or psychological and sociological theories, and place this alongside the host of technological facts and design theories that proliferate daily. For the shift in focus must imply a greater simplicity rather than an increased complexity; the creator of the man-made object must arrive at a different assessment of his own relationship with the world, a different evaluation of the nature and value of experience. Such is the distinguishing trait of all true artists and of "master architects" however diverse their work, for in it is embodied a clear and undeviating estimate of man and his relationship with his world, the shape and nature of experiences which are meaningful and ennobling. The heraldic dignity of Mies, whose architecture implies a monastic, ritualistic simplicity in a world of confused and nebulous experience; the respect for the "little man" which gives Aalto's work a simplicity and anonymity that is unassertive but intensely human; these are but two examples. It is a way of life that is formative.

The plagiarist sees only the form, being unable to feel the experience; he sees their work as the product of a limited design philosophy, a particular aesthetic, rather than a directed and committed belief.

It is obvious, then, that to arrive at this condition of belief does not depend on the acquisition of design skill or the management of technology, but on living toward an experiential understanding of man and man-made object. To suggest that this is wholly inborn and cannot be nurtured, that the "education" of an architect can only be factual and technological, or, far more dangerous, can only be based on a specific design philosophy, is analogous to maintaining that religious conversion is impossible, that a consistent and pervasive belief is limited to a select few. True artists are as rare as saints, but there can and must be a corpus of the creatively committed as well as of the faithful. Development lies in the lines of experience, the ability to enter into a live and meaningful relationship, a humanity where true living is meeting.[6] Such a condition is not fanciful, it is found in the intuitive and unaware folk community where a level of unconscious perfection is achieved through total commitment to direct experience, where all things are an "instant reality." Development does not, however, imply a reversion to the state of the primitive—though the thought and work of certain architects and theorists may suggest this—but rather a progression to a state of "super-consciousness"; not a denial of the rational but the harnessing of increasing knowledge to truly human ends.

Full identity, association, and therefore communication can only occur when there is a direct response to reality stemming from a quivering and fully awakened awareness undistorted by preconceived ideas. An awareness of qualities of form, texture, pattern, etc., that is a total psychosomatic response found in the unconscious state in the tiller of soil and the primitive, and in the unpatterned state of the child. It has for some decades been realized that this quality of awareness can be encouraged and nurtured quite independently from any design philosophy; "basic courses" are designed to break down preconceived association patterns and encourage direct committal to experience, and have done so since the early work of the Bauhaus. The process involves quite simply the reawakening of perception that has been atrophied by the very denial of experience that is characteristic of academic art education, and then by disciplining of the senses and of every means of relating. It demands a sloughing of academic ritual, denial of precise fact, and committal to the unknown and verbally inarticulate that is a condition of belief, an act of faith in the reality of experience. It is then that the man-made object becomes more than an objective form, a material existence, and is a live and present experience fully realized in meeting. This is analogous to the condition of "being" and applies not only to the work of art but to any object, however trivial, since it is wholly dependent on relationship rather than material worth.

The transition here to a "metaphysic" should not cause concern. For this direct identification through meeting is precisely that I-thou relationship defined by Martin Buber—the experiential relationship that cannot be explained, that must be experienced; the meeting of lovers, the moment out of time.[7] In fact, it is frequently maintained that such experience being necessarily inchoate—because defying verbal description—is safest relegated to the realm of sacred or profane love. The true artist would never allow such restriction. Indeed the process of "relating" through experience is a

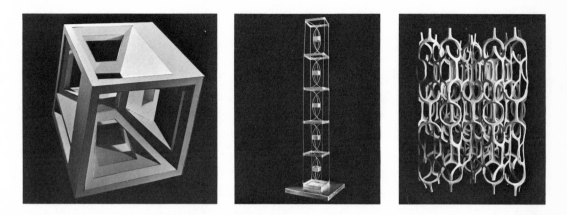

fundamental way of orienting, of becoming, of knowing. Knowledge and experience are not antitheses but complementaries, both to be developed with equal application.[8]

A creator who realizes this must automatically shift his focus to this interval between man and man-made object, for here in the experience lies his commitment and responsibility. His task is then conceived primarily as that of the evocation of experience with specific shape, direction, and intensity; with pattern and association. And in these terms the fundamental activity of the artist is that of creating relationships. For these to be re-experienced by the observer, a carefully established and controlled climate must be evoked; formal discipline such as rhythm, symmetry, proportion, is simply a means of articulating the relationship and not of provoking it. The artist in his unique fusion of disparates, in the tension of strange and unexpected relationships, can predict both direction and intensity if his concern has shifted to this new focus.

This then is intended purely as an indication of the climate of thought and feeling within which the architect today tackles increasingly complex problems; for without such fundamental reassessment his material is unwieldy and his problems are confusing. It enables a clearer vision of his world and a fuller realization of his responsibility. Specific design solutions developed within this field of force, guided by this belief in the experiential, achieve the proper regard for the particular condition without sacrificing the general experiential needs of identity, association, etc. It would be easy to conclude that an experiential emphasis was solely individualistic or atomistic, each situation existing purely in itself—in the unique and unqualified meeting. But this would be equivalent to maintaining a purely individualistic position in regard to human relationships; while the love between two people is *ipso facto* a unique experience, the condition has certain factors in common with other meetings which establish the concept of "loving." This coexistence of the universal and the particular alone justifies the general approach pursued here. Certain qualities and levels of identity and association are common to certain categories or modes of experience; it is these which can usually be studied outside the particular problem, and which can furnish the general principle, the experiential attitude, which must give shape and direction to the particular situation. It is the principle aim of social science to suggest just these general principles by a detailed study of particular situations. This might seem analogous to seeking the general and self-evident principle of love by the study of individual situations. It is here, however, that the analogy is illuminating. For it is most certainly no longer true to say that the general principles of an effective relationship are self-evident, that the fundamental needs of a satisfactory experience are recognized. It is only certain that in the intuitive condition of the cohesive community such needs are indeed satisfied. The problem today, however, is not simply one of rediscovering that which has been overlaid or disregarded by a conscious materialistic society[9] (though the recognition of the importance and continued relevance of primordial experiential requirements presents one face of the problem[10]). It is equally the correct evaluation of the contemporary forms in which these principles are or may be embodied, forms which frequently disguise, exaggerate, or misrepresent genuine experience.

The growth of experiential understanding does not rest therefore solely on increased awareness. This awareness must itself be discriminating, be capable of deducing from a plethora of involved experiences general identity or association needs. The full development of awareness will allow meaningful experience to lie in any area which succeeds in establishing basic identity needs and is therefore creatively formative. It is on this basis that the architect may find meaning and draw creative conclusions from any experiential relationship in which he may be involved, whether this relationship be with painting, music, poetry, sculpture, or even architecture. In seeking primordial patterns of identity he may indeed go direct to primitive communities for social study; in trying to identify with contemporary conditions of relating he may equally resort to his experiences of Pop art, abstract expressionism, comic or science fiction.[11]

Full awareness is therefore synonymous with developed critical judgment, judgment that selects first and foremost on the basis of a quality of relationship, the satisfaction of basic identity needs, free from the restriction of preconceptions, of rigid Gestalten. The stance of the architect, for instance, must be always unbiased yet critical and securely founded on experiential involvement. The full development of his awareness should ensure an openness to any experience in whatever field, and the use of any technique that will enable his experience to be turned to creative ends.

This suggests a creative alternative to distorted materialistic value judgments, prone to the vicissitudes of fashion change—the ideals of a sales-oriented society; equally a creative alternative to judgments based upon preconceived formal ideas that fail to recognize the breadth of contemporary vision in space and time. Materialism and formalism are normally regarded as mutually exclusive systems. The experiential focus represents an inclusive view that is no less concrete and specific, demanding as it does direct contact and involved relationship in contrast to the superficiality of the materialist and the remoteness of the theorist.

It is not denied, however, that some kind of accepted formal vocabulary is necessary for effective communication, and there is equally the need for the trivial, the transitory, and the fashionable. In this the man-made object is necessarily as diverse as the experiences of which man is capable. The individuated man accepts this situation not by an indiscriminate abandonment to piecemeal experience but by a recognition of the diversity of experience which is necessary to the full and balanced life. It is not the man-made object that is changed but the attitude, the quality of relationship. While the materialist regards the automobile as a status symbol and demands formal expression

of this fact, it does not mean that a denial of materialism must deny the automobile. However, a radical extension of modes of relationship does seem essential if such situations, so typical of our contemporary condition, are to be subsumed within this total experiential attitude to the man-made object. And against the background of the argument thus far, it seems quite natural to frame the contemporary dilemma in this way, otherwise, the problem of the machine-made would evoke a "William Morris" response, a denial of the possibility or sense of such extension.

For the primitive his wooden bowl is valued, fingered, felt, and known; a true man-made extension, his spoon a prehensile projection of his own anatomy. Each of his few possessions has a similar intense reality,[12] each is necessary and life-enhancing. It is surely experientially relevant to ask to what extent such identity can be offered by or demanded of the trivia of materialistic society, the paper plate, the plastic spoon. If identity depends wholly on scarcity, slowness, familiarization, frequent contact, then the contemporary urban environment denies all possibility of such experience. It is here in particular that modes of relationship are extended by new conditions of meeting—the new space-time conjunction dictated by movement. The contemporary environment, the rich assembly of man-made objects that structures it, has then a collective image generated by a bombardment of experience, an intensity created by sheer pressure and repetition, and by the lack of individual definition due to movement. Here most surely are radically different problems of identity, different categories of creative responsibility.

To the architect, all this is of direct concern. For the architect is involved in the creation of man-made objects comprising a shaped environment that must articulate collective and individual needs unfounded on traditional social patterns and traditional qualities of identity. He can be neither traditional—indulging in pseudo-folk vernacular and craft methods—nor individualistic—indulging in whims and gimmicks that appeal to a craving for change in itself, or satisfy inflated egos. The scale of his concern alone demands a collective creativity in which individualism is dangerous. The solution is not to be found simply in group design. But if an agreed experiential basis is achieved which takes precedence over particular concerns of style or construction, and if the primary concern lies in relationship, then the climate of creativity will be automatically altered and a unity of purpose ensured.

It is naturally difficult to envisage an ideal which suggests such a fundamentally different estimate of the creative method; but that other attitudes to creativity exist is amply demonstrated. The Indian Hindu and the Japanese Zen denial of self, the affirmation of the artist as a vehicle for a pervasive creative force, comes close to the condition of humility and conscious technical perfection that is demanded of the contemporary situation. It becomes the duty of the creator to prepare and perfect himself, so that the creative force may be channeled through a worthy vessel. A new anonymity that does not deny the delight of the artist in creation nor assume the unself-consciousness of the folk artist, must inevitably seem a strange and alien attitude to ears attuned to the song of the cult hero.

I have suggested that the dissolution of rigid compartments, of fixed attitudes, of materialistic or formalist systems, is an essential need if the problems of contemporary society are to be resolved; and that this does not imply an abandonment to anarchy simply denying the validity of these positions. I have tried to indicate that a focus on the interval between man and man-made object—on the relationship between—discovers a positive attitude, a dynamic awareness that subsumes apparent opposites, reconciles incompatibles; and that this experiential basis involves also a fundamental shift in the attitude toward creativity itself. Such conclusions seem to arise naturally from any attempt to trace current tendencies, to trace the groping of artists and architects in their attempt to face genuine creative demands, pressing problems in shaping the man-made object today—from the resettlement of a backward community to the shaping of a new urban environment. Indeed, every creative problem is seen in a new light when regarded in these terms of shaping experience, of developing a particular relationship between man and object. To take but one example: the task of urban planning. In order to achieve the necessary consistency of attitude it becomes essential to inquire into the kind of experience structure that is already common in the urban environment in order that a new coherency may be planned for. Obviously this is a case for direct sociological research of the kind that has already been carried out on the "perceptual image of the city."[13] But it is characteristic of this shift in focus that anything which enlightens and extends experience is of value in developing the true creative climate. And so it may well be just as valuable to study the embodied experience structure of the visual artist as it is to study the behavior patterns of the typical city dweller. For the artist may reveal with greater sensitivity and through heightened experience qualities of relationship which are evasive, inarticulate or unconscious. I am thinking here of certain contemporary paintings and sculptures that reveal a species of urban image as having especial meaning and significance, and that indicate the status of the individual man-made objects that crowd our world, and the kind of relationships which the artist is able to establish with them.

In such work the kaleidoscope of materials and sensations that are a twentieth-century commonplace—none felt deeply but with a collective impact, none individually articulated but asserted by the massive pressure of quantity—are fused into figures of almost totemic intensity, composed "as found" into structures of heroic presumption. They exist as collective images; their individual and individualistic forms are fused but not as wholes, as clear identities, rather as scraps half seen, obliquely experienced at speed, in a hurry . . . "quick now, here now, always." All this is simply achieved

by the direct assembly of trivia, the elevation of the everyday and the familiar to a level demanding attention; machine and machine-made are re-used, re-structured in a way that creates personalities, fetishes, totems; that generates a life-force and yet denies the life of the constituent elements; that demands a new kind of identity, a different quality of experience. Or again a forced precision, a hard edge, may be used to give an unmerited clarity and boldness to the supremely trivial; and this prominence demands some kind of acceptance, not as an ideal but as unself-conscious, brash, and even vulgar elements of life.

Such work reveals ways of relating categories of awareness that must influence the way in which the man-made object is actually seen, for, as with all art, an extension of awareness is effected. One kind of conclusion that might be drawn is that the aim of the urban planner would be to plan for and contain the trivia of which such images are compounded; that he should recognize the fact that many urban images are indeed images of accretion, images of irresponsibility, since close identity is largely denied and frequently discouraged.

At the other extreme from this transmutation of contemporary trivia there are artists who deny outright the validity of the individual man-made object as provocative of deep relationships, or meaningful experiences. Their work seeks to evoke images of primordial intensity, experiences that are beyond or before time yet are fundamental to all men; these are really basic statements of association and identity that existed before verbal communication and with the force of a mandala. Strange chthonic powers brood over these canvases, they seem to celebrate a time when the sun was low and blood-red and thought first formed black upon a scrabbled sky. They are moving proof of the continued existence of gods that have long since been submerged by materialistic trivia and yet cannot so easily be forgotten or ignored. Again the urban planner would do well to allow experiences such as these provoke. His structure must be bold and coherent enough to contain the collective images of urban trivia, and this can only be achieved if he acknowledges those forces that are out of time. Certain architects have expressed such needs in more concrete terms as part of a planning credo, but the essential is an attitude of mind, a climate of thought and feeling that is fundamentally experiential.

Such suggestions as these, drawn from all kinds of experience, spawn questions that are quite unlike those which emerge from a particular aesthetic philosophy, a particular design formula. For instance, in terms of the problem of the urban environment, and the new aspects raised by the two art manifestations mentioned above, the questions which emerge might follow a course such as: what kind of man-made object relationship do these artistic manifestations reflect? do they suggest modes of relationship which the environmentalist should acknowledge, plan for, and develop in his work? For in this case the work of the artist makes use of environmental chaos, comes to terms with the experiential world of neon, chrome, and sex. Does this mean that acceptance is implicit, that this is the "stuff" of a live society? or again does this represent a shallow argument for the vulgar? The fact that the environment planned according to ideal notions, to theoretic scientific requirements, is wholly without humanity raises further questions: is there not a need to come to terms with this vulgar and transient element and with the myriad products of a machine age and an acquisitive society? Is any such assessment possible or necessary? is it rather chance (controlled chance) that should be allowed to compromise the ideal? Or again, does the preoccupation with sensation (experience relationship), rather than object, indicate a different attitude toward creativity, as I have already suggested? Finally, is the kind of experience relationship possible or desirable in a brash materialistic world necessarily superficial? have we not simply to readjust our vision and our awareness, initially content to delight quite simply in the actual involvement, the meeting?

Similarly, the kind of conclusions made from such questioning are also of a different order. In a complex modern environment the kind of deep involvement with the man-made object, so typical of the primitive society, is impossible and indeed dangerous. The intimate focus is necessarily limited to certain restricted and often piecemeal relationships, around which an unlimited and uncommitted world of experiences flickers. There may be momentary and often ludicrous attempts to elevate trifles—by a surreal conjunction or by isolation—but our way of experience may itself encourage a blurred relationship, an undefined Gestalten. A right quality of relationship cannot imply a single fixed and immutable man-object situation, for this is death to experience and neither element in the equation is static if the relationship between is live and new each moment. For a given situation, however, there must be certain potential relationships which can be predicted, and others which may be regarded as impossible and outside the field of focus. Again, certain relationships must ever retain a quality of remoteness without in any way being superficial—a coral island on an air route, a neon message on a high building, a turnpike landscape. Shaped environment may give context and structure to this kind of relationship so that it is no longer superficial, its true value is discovered; only then is the fleeting, the conglomerate related to the immutable and individual, with each realizing the potential of a relationship by first accepting the level of meeting.

Planning, design, the creation of the man-made object in terms of experience must imply a shift in emphasis from formal to experiential ideals, seeking in a dynamic relationship to provoke feeling responses which expand and enhance life. Then the criterion of judgment for the man-made object will not be that of craft technique, finish, etc., or efficient function fulfillment; it will not be that of satisfaction of desire, or of status, but the experience provoked through meeting. A satisfactory experience may in fact depend primarily on efficient function—a knife that cuts—, on the creation of a feeling of pleasure, but the core is that total feeling response, that identity and communion which is true meeting, when the "real" is discovered first hand.

I have tried to indicate the sort of thinking in which the architect today is liable to indulge. Where it is vulnerable, where it trespasses blindly across the domains of other disciplines, it reveals the pressing need for clearer thought, for a more direct dialogue. The response to such necessarily loose argument should not be to retreat into our prescribed compartments—where we "belong"—but to venture forth boldly, to seek a closer understanding, an agreed language, a unity of purpose.[14] As far as the architect is concerned, the sole purpose must be to further the creative act of shaping—the object, the environment: and the ground for such meeting lies in the interval between man and the object he shapes, in the experiential relationship that is established when they are confronted.

1. "Habitus": here I am forced to a term used by the medieval scholastics to convey the total psychosomatic discipline. *Cf*. Jacques Maritain, *Art and Scholasticism* (translated by Joseph W. Evans), New York, Scribner (1962).

2. On the existentialist position with reference to value that is adopted here I have been rather free with the close reasoning of Jean-Paul Sartre, *Being and Nothingness*, New York, Citadel (1964).

3. In architectural education this is reflected in fundamental changes in curricula and the inclusion of certain aspects of social science, psychology, etc. The fusion of disciplines into a Department of Environmental Studies at the University of California is typical.

4. *Cf*. Rudolf Arnheim, "A Review of Proportion," in *The Journal of Aesthetics and Art Criticism* (September, 1955), and reprinted in *Module, Proportion, Symmetry, Rhythm* (Vision + Value Series, Gyorgy Kepes, editor), New York, George Braziller (1966); and John Summerson, *Heavenly Mansions,* New York, W. W. Norton (1963).

5. Kevin Lynch, *The Image of the City*, Cambridge, Mass., Massachusetts Institute of Technology Press and Harvard University Press (1960).

6. "All real living is meeting," from Martin Buber, *I and Thou*, in *The Writings of Martin Buber* (Will Herberg, editor), Cleveland, Meridian Books (1956); *I and Thou*, New York, Scribner (1958).

7. Buber, *op. cit.*

8. "It has been a common illusion that the objects of science are more 'real' than the objects of common experience." Louis Arnaud Reid, *Ways of Knowledge and Experience,* Oxford University Press (1961), p. 31.

9. *"There is only the fight to recover what has been lost/ And found and lost again and again."* T. S. Eliot, "East Coker," in *The Four Quartets*, New York, Harcourt (1963).

10. ". . . What should be their shared facilities—the value equivalent of the village pump; continually questioning the arbitrariness of existing solutions. This is the basic step of the ecological approach to the problem of habitat." Alison and Peter Smithson in *Architectural Design* (June, 1955), p. 187.

11. See comments and quotes of the Archigram Group in *Architectural Design* (Nov., 1965), p. 559.

12. *"Nothing is beautiful until it has reality, and art is the apprehension of the real."* John Wain, "A boisterous poem about Poetry," Part 10, in *Weep Before God*, New York, St. Martin's Press (1961).

13. Lynch, *op. cit.*

14. The first work to tackle this problem comprehensively is: Norberg-Schulz, *Intentions in Architecture*, London, Allen and Unwin (1963).

The natural effect of any new technology is to create a new environment for itself. In effect, an environment is a special organization of available energies. As an energy system, an environment is a process. It reprocesses the earlier environments. Old environments are the nutriment of new ones. As they are assimilated by the new energy system, the older systems are transformed into art forms. From the cliché environment to the archetypal content, the new environmental system turns the old environments into anti-environments. That is one way of perceiving what a work of art is. Art as an anti-environment is an indispensable means of perception, for environments, as such, are imperceptible. Their power to impose their ground rules on our perceptual life is so complete that there is no scope for dialogue or interface. Hence the need for art or anti-environments.

Indeed, the power of the environment to be invisible and to condition, or to brainwash subjects, was what Pavlov stressed in his work, according to the recent investigations of Erwin Straus.[1] The message of Pavlov was that the stimulus cannot be a conditioner. Only a totally controlled environment effects conditioning. Such is also the message of Jacques Ellul in his book, *Propaganda*.[2] Ideology, he says, is not propaganda. Only the simultaneous use of all the available environmental technologies is propaganda. The Western world, locked in habits of fragmented and specialized perception, ignores both the meaning of Pavlov and of Ellul by insisting on translating their vision into the terms of the old technologies. From the time that Neolithic man-the-planter began to create environments one at a time by specialist extensions of his hands and arms and feet, men have always looked at a new environment as if it were the old one. We can never see the Emperor's new clothes, but we are staunch admirers of his old garb. Only small children and artists are sensuously apt to perceive the new environment. Small children and artists are anti-social beings who are as little impressed by the established mores as they are conditioned by the new.

In his *Uncommon Law*, Alan P. Herbert records a British legal case that concerned the publication of Sunday newspapers. Evidence was brought that "what is called 'news' is always an anti-social and disturbing act; that 'news' consists, as to ninety per cent, of the records of human misfortunes, unhappiness and wrongdoing, as to nine per cent of personal advertisement . . ."[3]

It has often mystified readers of the press that real news is bad news. Good news is simply not news. The ads are full of good news. Good news is a repeat of the old environment, while bad news is a probe into the new environment. Bad news reveals the lines of force in an environment, while good news tends merely to picture the situation passively. Thus the Nielsen ratings in press stories are even more whimsically destructive and sudden than those in entertainment.

It does help to look at the newspaper as a direct, exploratory probe into the environment. Seen in this light, there is more meaning in the aesthetic bonds between the poet, the sleuth, and even the criminal. For James Bond, Humphrey Bogart, Rimbaud, and Hemingway are all figures who explore the shifting frontiers of morals and society. They are engaged in detecting the social environment by probing and transgression. For to probe is to cross boundaries of many kinds; to discover the patterns of new environments requires a rigorous study and inventory of sensuous effects. The components of new environments cannot be discovered directly. Edgar Allan Poe's detective, Dupin, is an aesthete.

The aesthetes were the first to use the senses consciously and systematically as probes into the environment. Walter Pater's injunction, "To burn always with a hard gemlike flame," referred to the action of the plumber's blowtorch, a technical innovation of his day.

As the visual gradient built up in the culture and technology of the seventeenth and eighteenth centuries, much accelerated by the printing press, man lost much of the power to deal with the non-visual factors in experience.[4] The visual bias of our culture even today is such as to create a great gap between literary and scientific sectors. For the world of electric circuitry is only incidentally related to visual factors. And *The Philosophical Impact of Contemporary Physics* by Milič Čapek[5] reveals the handicaps confronting even the Einsteins in their unconscious commitments to visual culture.

The eighteenth century went so far in developing the visual gradient of its culture that realism became acceptable. The putting of the ordinary outer environment inside books and theaters for inspection and enjoyment was to go even further in the nineteenth century. But in the middle of the nineteenth century the birth of modern art occurred in several arts at once. Whereas the Romantics had developed outer landscape in poetry and painting as a means of defining and controlling inner mental states, the symbolists, by fragmenting the realistic Romantic landscapes, were able to use the pieces as heuristic probes. The probes were used to explore and define the inner landscapes that had eluded merely visual organization and detection. A similar reversal from outer to inner modalities occurred in the rise of the stream-of-consciousness technique in poetry and fiction alike. Paradoxically, stream of consciousness offered the reader a means of making rather than of matching. By pushing cinematic and photographic imagery flow to an extreme, the poets discovered the means of making a world in which all the senses participated at once. Such had been the earlier vision of the "Romantic Image," as Frank Kermode has shown in his book of that title.[6] It is a vision that is fully realized in "Among School Children" by W. B. Yeats. As the visual gradient of the Renaissance reached its ultimate development, the poets, from Blake and Coleridge to Hopkins and Yeats, strove to restore the unity of the imaginative life by creating a multisensuous interplay. Yeats wrote:

> I have spent my life in clearing out of poetry every phrase written for the eye, and bringing all back to syntax that is for the ear alone. . . . "Write for the ear," I thought, so that you may be instantly understood as when actor or folk singer stands before an audience.[7]

If poets and artists began to revolt a century ago against the merely visual and pictorial organization of space and experience, it is notable that the camera has revolted likewise. Cinema is not merely visual, being the joining of eye and foot. In *Our World from the Air,* E. A. Gutkind[8] has revealed the entirely structural and nonobjective qualities that are released from the terrestrial surface when camera joins the airplane. At 35,000 feet the earth belongs to Picasso, and abstract *making.* At 12,000 feet it is still in the hands of representational art, or the modes of matching. At night the urban landscape belongs to Seurat and Rouault. It is a world of light *through* rather than of light *on.* It is the world of TV and reverse perspective in which the viewer is the vanishing point.

Such extensions of our faculties have immediate effects on our habits of perception. This is called "negative feedback," or learned responses to new situations. The photograph revolutionized the human image as much as it changed the patterns and spaces of our cities. Indeed, the photograph gave us a push in the direction of the programmed environment. As our data become more inclusive and ecological, we naturally begin to look at the environment as a huge teaching machine that can translate us out of the human dimension altogether. It then occurs to us that we might be able to translate, or program, the environment before it translates us. Oceanographers, confronting the extravagant life of the sea, are yet mindful of the equilibrium among its creatures and components. It is the maintenance of this equilibrium that initiates trains of actions and effects of "mindless ferocity." Such had been the first theories of political economy when human factors were subordinated to the Newtonian image of Nature. As we approach the stage of programming the environment itself, it becomes natural to interrupt and suspend the "mindless ferocity" of Nature by anticipating causes with consequences. It is a revolution well under way, and it is parallel to a similar revolution in education. A great shift from instruction to discovery is beginning in education. It is the shift from matching to making, from blueprint to heuristic probe. It is based on the same kind of knowledge that earlier had enabled the engineer to predict the behavior of skyscrapers, bombs, and rockets. We can begin to program the planet itself by understanding the actions under and above its mantle.

So little did the ancients know of the make-up of their terrestrial environment that they misnamed the planet. Had they been able to perceive the extent of the waters on the earth (70.8 per cent of its surface) they might well have called it Oceanus. But their perceptions of their earthly environment were no more inadequate or deluded than the perceptions of men in other ages and cultures. It might be well to consider briefly the role of the artist in correcting the bias of environmental perception.

If we note the artistic response of the Romantics to the first mechanical and industrial age, it will help to explain the artistic response to the first electronic age. For with electric circuitry we may have come to the end of the Neolithic time of the Planter and the Wheel. The electronic age is again the age of the Hunter, the nonspecialist, who can probe the entire environment. New data-retrieval systems make this total probing more and more natural.

James Joyce published *Finnegan's Wake* in 1939, revealing the return of the tribal cycle for electronic man and opening the entire world of language as a Phoenix Playhouse of dramatic metamorphoses. The artistic response to the age of circuitry has been to portray new dimensions of human interdependence and new patterns of human identity. The unconscious that had long been the environment of consciousness has become the content of modern artistic awareness. The Romantics, on the other hand, had responded to the first mechanical environment of railways and factories by a nostalgic dream of the preceding agrarian technology. Has it always occurred this way? Does the content of each new environment have to be the old environment? Does the new organization of energy that is a new environment automatically process the old environment into an archetypal ideal of art? The television environment has steadily upgraded the old movie forms into sentimentally valued art forms. The medieval world got the same treatment from the Gutenberg technology. If technological changes create new environments, or new processes of energy organization, what is to be the process of the new satellite environments on our perception and experience?

It is a common observation that in the space age we do much of our lab work outside the planet. That is just a way of looking at the new environment in terms of the old one. For radio, telescopes, and space capsules are not new content for the old situation. In the same way, the computer is not a new mechanical gadget for pepping up the old mechanical environment. The computer is not mechanical at all. Electric circuitry is an organic thing, an extension of our nervous system. Our natural impulse is to ignore the environmental aspects and to try to fit it into the old situation in the style of "horseless carriage" and "wireless." But our natural response is quite helpless and irrelevant, as the history of technology testifies.

The capsule and the satellite have created a new environment for our planet. The planet is now the content of the new spaces created by the new technology. Instead of being an environment in time, the earth itself has become a probe in space. That is, the planet has become an anti-environment, an art form, an extension of consciousness, yielding new perception of the new man-made environment. Whereas the mechanical environment turned the old agrarian world into an art form, the electric technology enables us to mime or simulate the old planetary environment in our capsules. As Buckminster Fuller has pointed out, "the rocket capsule that will keep man living successfully in space for protracted periods . . . will be the first 'scientific dwelling' in history."[9] Science, quite as much as art, is concerned with the construction of anti-environments. In the electric age the anti-environments of science incorporate the nervous system. They become "responsive environments," or probes. With electric circuitry we cannot only program the entire environment responsively as a work of art, we can include the learning process in the environment itself.

In his *Poetics* (Chapter IV, 1448b), Aristotle reminded us that mimesis is the process by which all men learn. He alluded to the process of making by which our perceptions simulate within us the environment that we encounter outside ourselves. It is this learning and making process that, by electric circuitry, is being extended beyond our central nervous system. The next phase of this extension will naturally concern the action of making consciousness technologically. What we have called education in recent centuries has consisted in visiting or in simulating as many earlier environments and cultures as possible. Language is unrivaled in providing the actual sensuous modalities of other environments, with their unique ground rules. Electric circuitry can become a means to bypass language and plug directly into other modes of consciousness. Already the artists have shown us the means to this end with their strategy of the "objective correlative," or an inclusive experiential control. It is a method for anticipating the effects of a contrived situation that Edgar Allan Poe previewed in his essay, "The Philosophy of Composition." Instead of being concerned with the content of the work, Poe's method points to our own time when it is possible to include the environment in the content.

With electric circuitry, all the mechanical enterprises of mankind tend to acquire reverse characteristics. Just as the educational establishment tends to shift its stress from instruction to discovery with the audience directly involved in the learning processes, so all mechanical industry tends to abandon packaging in favor of the tailor-made or custom-built service for the individual. This pattern begins to emerge in computer design procedures in architecture. It appears quite spectacularly in the world of the book and of publishing with the advent of xerography. The book was the first mass-produced object. It was the first repeatable and uniform product. The process by which this kind of product was achieved was a process soon extended to many other forms of making. The process consists in the extreme fragmentation of the ancient craft of the scribe. Printing from movable type is not only an analytic procedure of fragmentation, but it fathered similar fragmentation in many areas of human perception and human action.

It is precisely on this process of analytic fragmentation that all the fabrics of modern production, marketing, and pricing were built. It is a process that dissolves with the advent of electric circuitry. The dissolution of this process can be illustrated from the effects of xerography on book publication. Xerography makes the reader both author and publisher in tendency. The highly centralized activity of publishing naturally breaks down into extreme decentralism when anybody can, by means of xerography, assemble printed, or written, or photographic materials which can be supplied with sound tracks.

There are many electric information services at present that permit individuals to phone for printed data on any subject whatever. Computers are ready to go to work on their specific problem, or interest. Bibliographies and printed materials from many parts of the world can be made available to the individual in a few hours. The whole tendency of xerography is to transform the book into a tailor-made, custom-built service. The way in which the book is ceasing to be a mass-produced object or commodity provides a very good index to the changing aspect of the world itself as it becomes a responsive information environment. As the specific individual needs become paramount in the new book-making, the public is drawn into the book-making process. Artists have, during the past century, been vividly aware of the ever increasing measure in which the audience shares in the creative process. This is an aspect of the "mass audience" that is frequently deplored and misunderstood by the representatives of the old mechanical culture and environment. Such people tend to see the mass audience as the mere obliteration of old landmarks, and of individual differences. They pay no attention to the increasingly creative awareness of people who are deeply involved in one another by means of electric circuitry. They are engaged in the ancient routine of regarding the patterns of the previous environment with nostalgic reverence.

The individualism of the mechanical culture and environment was paid for at the cost of much alienation from man, and work, and society. It was also accompanied by an almost total denial of participation in the creative process on the part of the public. The mechanical culture and environment produced the spectator and the consumer instead of the participant and co-creator. Mechanized specialism permitted high virtuosity in the shaping of the art object, but such objects were denied any real role in the social life. They were classified as "art" and made peripheral to society and to individual consciousness alike. "We have no art," say the Balinese; "We do everything as well as possible." In the same way, art as a classified activity dissolves with the advent of electric circuitry. The art object is replaced by participation in the art process. This is the essential meaning of electric circuitry and responsive environments. The artist leaves the Ivory Tower for the Control Tower, and abandons the shaping of art objects in order to program the environment itself as a work of art.

It is human consciousness itself that is the great artifact of man. The making and shaping of consciousness from moment to moment is the supreme artistic task of all individuals. To qualify and to perfect this process on a world environmental scale is the inherent potential of each new technology.

1. Erwin Straus, *The Primary World of the Senses,* New York, Free Press of Glencoe (1962).
2. Jacques Ellul, *Propaganda,* New York, Knopf (1965).
3. Alan P. Herbert, *Uncommon Law,* London, Methuen (1935), p. 14.
4. See E. J. Dijksterhuis, *The Mechanization of the World Picture,* Oxford, Oxford University Press (1961), pp. 418 ff.
5. Milič Čapek, *The Philosophical Impact of Contemporary Physics,* Princeton, N.J., Van Nostrand (1961).
6. Frank Kermode, *Romantic Image,* New York, Chilmark Press (1963).
7. Quoted by M. C. Bradbrook in his book *English Dramatic Form,* London, Chatto and Windus (1965), p. 125.
8. E. A. Gutkind, *Our World from the Air,* London, Chatto and Windus (1952).
9. R. Buckminster Fuller, in *World Resources Inventory,* Carbondale, Southern Illinois University Press, Phase 1 (1965), Document 3, p. 90.

CHRISTOPHER ALEXANDER

FROM A SET OF FORCES TO A FORM

There are more and more man-made objects in our environment. Each one is made to meet certain needs, but unfortunately they often fail to meet the needs. This raises the question: "Given a set of needs, how can we generate a form which meets those needs?"

In this paper I shall describe three fundamentally different ways of doing this: by numerical methods, by analog methods, and by relational methods. Numerical methods and analog methods are in common use. Indeed, most of the research now being done on "systematic" methods of design is based on these methods. However, I believe that they are almost entirely unsuited to environmental design: they are far too simple. The complexity of the needs which enter into the design of an object like a house demands much more general, and more powerful, methods.

In the last section I shall deal with a class of methods which I call relational methods. I believe they are, in principle, capable of generating form even in answer to the great complexity of human needs. But they are so far almost unexplored. I have written this paper in the hope that it may persuade some of the people now working on numerical and analog methods to shift their attention to relational methods.

Let us begin by extending the concept of a "need."

The concept of a need has several faults. It can easily be unobjective, it gives no indication of the kind of form which satisfies the need and, worst of all, it is too narrow. It leaves out many other factors which must influence the form of buildings: the force of gravity, the tendency for heat to flow across a temperature gradient, the fact that people tend to walk in straight lines, the social forces which make it necessary for a housewife to keep a "tidy room" for visiting strangers, the economic forces which cause a steady drift of population from rural into urban areas, the processes of production and distribution which force builders to use pre-assembled factory components, and the deeper psychological demands of human nature.

I shall therefore replace the concept of need, by the concept of "force." A force is an invention. It is an invented motive power which summarizes some recurrent and inexorable tendency which we observe in nature.

All systems, whether they are individual human organisms, or social systems, or mechanical systems, share the following property: when in certain states, they have inexorable tendencies to seek certain other states. If the system is human, we summarize these tendencies in terms of needs. If the system is mechanical, we summarize the tendencies in terms of Newtonian forces. If the system is thermodynamic, we summarize the tendencies in terms of thermodynamic potential. If the system is social, we summarize the tendencies in terms of social forces. Etc., etc.

The fact that people need a certain light level for reading, summarizes the fact that, if they have the opportunity, they tend to switch the light on, or to dim the lights, or to move toward the window, when they find it hard to read.[1]

The force of gravity summarizes the inexorable tendency for two large masses to move toward each other.

Thermodynamic potential summarizes the inexorable tendency for heat to flow across a temperature gradient (like that between the inside of a building and the outside).[2]

The fact that people walk in straight lines, summarizes their inexorable tendency to take the shortest path between two points.[3]

When we speak of a woman's need to protect herself symbolically against invasion, we mean to summarize the fact that she tends to enclose herself—for instance, with elaborate window curtains.[4]

These kinds of tendency, and many many other kinds, all play their part in shaping the environment. We must therefore choose a single word to summarize them. I have chosen the word *force*.

In order to define a tendency we must define:

1. The exact circumstances under which the force arises.
2. The exact conditions which the force is seeking.

Forces generate form. In the case of certain simple natural systems, this is literally true. In the case of complex, man-made systems, it is a metaphor. Let us look at a simple system first.

When a constant wind blows across a sandy surface, it forms wave-like ripples in the sand (Fig. 1). There are five forces at work.[5]

Fig. 1. Sand ripples. Reproduced from Vaughan Cornish, *Ocean Waves*, Cambridge University Press (1934).

1. If there is any irregularity in the surface, the number of grains arriving on its windward slope (the slope facing the wind) is greater than the number arriving on the leeward slope (the slope facing away from the wind). The windward slope therefore tends to "catch" grains, and to grow.

2. The wind picks up grains and carries them a certain distance. For a given wind speed, this distance tends to be approximately constant.

3. The wind picks up more grains on a windward slope than on a leeward slope, and since it carries the majority of grains the same distance, any irregularity tends to be repeated one "path length" downwind.

4. When the grains land, their impact pushes other grains forward, causing creep. The impact is usually not enough to carry a large grain beyond the crest of a ripple, but it will carry small grains beyond the crest, so that the larger grains tend to accumulate at the crests.

5. On the crests, where the wind velocity is higher than in the dips, small grains tend to get blown off, and only heavy grains stay put.

These five forces make any level surface or any unevenly spaced pattern of bumps unstable. The slightest bump will grow into a ripple; and the ripples will repeat at regular intervals downwind, so that gradually a "wavelike" pattern of ripples is built up. With the wind blowing, the level sand surface is an unstable form because it gives rise to forces which ultimately destroy it. The rippled form is stable because the forces which it gives rise to maintain the form.

Let us now contrast this simple system with a complex system in the man-made world—a family and the house it lives in.

Although its evolution has made it partially stable, this system is still, in a larger sense, unstable. Periodically, it gives rise to forces whose repercussions threaten to destroy the harmony and stability of the whole.[6]

People in the house will tend to try and escape from neighbor noise. But the house may not allow them to escape it, so the tendency has repercussions. People close bedroom windows and make the bedroom stuffy. They turn up the volume of the radio to drown the noise, making more noise in the neighborhood. Or the tendency goes underground altogether, until it finds an outlet in bad temper.

Again, people tend to try and store things on open level surfaces at about waist height. When there is no provision for this tendency, things get put on the kitchen stove and start a fire; or they get stored in a forgotten place and cannot be found when wanted; or, they get left on narrow window sills, and then knocked down and broken.

The forces which are not provided for do not disappear. They always find an outlet in an unexpected way. The deeper psychological and social forces, if not provided for, can easily have repercussions which lead to drastic kinds of instability. They do not, of their own accord, create a stable state.

Unlike the forces in a simple system, which always steer the system to a stable state, the forces in a complex man-made system are often impotent. The tendency to escape neighbor noise does not, of its own accord, create a quiet building. The tendency to store things on open level surfaces does not provide a house with large amounts of open level surface.

This is the basic difference between a natural object and a man-made object. A natural object is formed directly by the forces which act upon it and arise within it. A man-made object is also formed by certain forces; but there are many other latent forces which have no opportunity to influence the form directly, with the result that the system in which the object plays a part may be unstable. The form can be made stable with respect to all these forces only by artificial means. The most usual artificial method is that known as "design," in which an individual designer tries to generate the form

intuitively. But "design" is only a particular way of doing this; there are other ways. We may state the problem of design, in its most general form, in two parts:

1. Given a system, how can we assess the forces which act upon it and arise within it?
2. Given a set of forces, how can we generate a form which will be stable with respect to them?

I shall not deal with the difficult problem of assessing forces here. Let us assume that they have been established by some reliable and objective means.[7] There are then various ways of generating form from them. I shall now describe three ways of generating form.

I. NUMERICAL METHODS

All numerical methods of generating form rely on three essentials:

1. Each "force" can be represented by the variation of a one-dimensional numerical variable. One of these seeks minimization (or maximization). The others are held constant, and are called constraints.
2. Equations or inequalities relate the values of the different variables to the configuration of the system and to one another.
3. There exists a theorem, or an algorithm, which defines the configuration in which the chosen force reaches its minimum (or maximum) value, under the constraints provided by the others.

Here are three examples of numerical methods:

The calculus of variations. The calculus of variations defines curves and surfaces on which some chosen integral reaches a maximum or minimum.[8]

Suppose, for instance, we have a system in which material slides down a chute, from one point to another, and suppose there is a tendency to minimize the time it takes the material to slide down the chute. The time can be expressed as an integral along the curve. The calculus of variations then shows that in order to minimize time, the chute must have the form of a cycloid.

Plant layout analysis and linear programing. Given any organization in which there is a lot of movement, like a hospital or an industrial plant, there will be certain tendencies for people and materials to move from one department to another; there will also be a tendency to try and cut down the total amount of daily movement in the organization as a whole.

The (nearly) best layout for such an organization can be generated by a simple algorithm. This algorithm is based on the idea that you can compute the total daily movement, for any given layout, and then make successive improvements in the layout, by exchanging departments, until no exchange of departments leads to an improvement. This method has been widely used for laying out of both industrial plants and hospitals.[9]

The Michell Theorem. In the design of a load-bearing frame structure, the principle forces are the loads themselves (with their magnitude, position, and direction specified), and the tendency to try and reduce the weight of the structure to a minimum.

A theorem by A. G. M. Michell makes it possible to generate the form of the least-weight structure almost uniquely, from a specification of the loads. The theorem shows that all the members of the least-weight structure must lie on one of two families of orthogonal curves (the compression members on one family, the tension members on the other), and places strong restrictions on these families of curves.[10]

For example, in the case of a simple cantilever, carrying a single load, the families of curves are near spirals, as shown in Fig. 2; and the least-weight cantilever which they generate is the fish-like structure illustrated in Fig. 3.[11]

These kinds of methods are beautiful as far as they go. But they are very limited. There is no guarantee that the forms they generate are stable, since it is likely, indeed, almost certain, that there will be other forces in the system which have not been represented. The Michell theorem, though it minimizes the weight of the structure, does not take into account the need to use steel sections which can easily be transported, or the fact that the cantilever will need periodic repainting. The hospital layout, though it minimizes movement, does not take into account the patients' need to feel secure in the hospital, or the need for conditions which speed up

cure. We must remember that numerical methods only work for forces which can be represented by the optimization of a single one-dimensional numerical variable. Most of the subtler human forces cannot be.

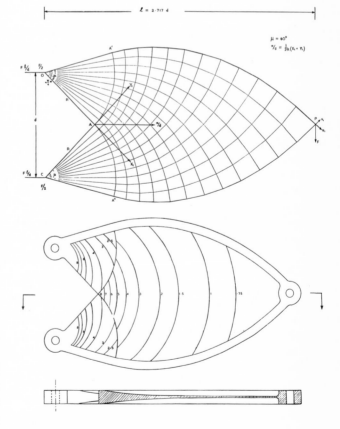

Fig. 2. Drawing for a simple cantilever.

Fig. 3. Drawing for a least-weight cantilever.

II. ANALOG METHODS

Analog methods actually generate form physically. As we know, the forces which occur in a system are often too weak to take the system to a stable state, of their own accord. It is sometimes possible to find a second system, which is a model or analog of the first, in which the forces model the forces of the first system, but are this time strong enough to take the system to a stable state. If the analog is well chosen, the form of this stable state will also be a stable form for the original system.

Analog methods rely on one essential: each force can be represented by some "active" force in the analog.

Here are three examples of analog methods:

The use of weights and strings to locate an elevator. Perhaps the simplest analog device of all is the use of weights and strings to generate the best position for an elevator on an office floor.[12] The analog consists of a board with holes drilled in it, one for each office, in its proper plan position. A piece of string is threaded through each hole. The lower end of each string has a weight tied to it. This weight is proportional to the number of people going to and from the office. At their upper ends all the strings are tied together. If the weights are allowed to hang free, the tension in each string is an active force which corresponds to the force of people's movement to and from the elevator. These active forces will move the knot to the most stable position for the elevator.

Antonio Gaudi's models for the Guell chapel.[13] Gaudi used analog devices to generate the form of stone load-bearing structures. The forces which actually operate in these structures are compressions, and are not, of their own accord, able to generate stable forms. Gaudi used upside-down wire-model analogs in which wires stand for columns, hanging bags of lead shot stand for the eventual compressing loads, and tensions stand for compressions. The tensions are able to pull the wires into a stable form (Fig. 4). This wire form, when turned upside-down, and made of stone, is stable under the original compressions (Fig. 5).

The experimental use of lightweight furniture. My third example of an analog is an actual living room. The forces at work within a living room are complex: tendencies for people to move through the room on certain paths, tendencies for people talking to sit close together, tendencies for people to move into positions where the draft is least, and to where the light is best, and to where they face the fire. . .

Under normal circumstances the furniture in a room is so heavy that these forces are powerless to move it. However, they can be made temporarily active. When I recently bought a house, instead of starting with permanent furniture in the living room, I started with lightweight bamboo stools for seats and tables. With these bamboo pieces in it, the room itself became an analog, the forces became temporarily active, and could push and kick the system from one state to another. After a few weeks, as people used them, the pieces fell into a stable pattern. This pattern defined the best configuration for the permanent furniture.

Again, these kinds of methods are beautiful as far as they go. But, like numerical methods, they are very limited. The wire model contains no force which represents the need for adequate light. The furniture analog contains no force which represents the need for easy cleaning. Analog methods only work for forces which can be represented by some "active" counterpart. Most of the subtler human forces cannot be.

Fig. 4. Canvas and wire model for Guell chapel. The photograph of the model, which is actually suspended from the ceiling, is here reproduced upside down.

Fig. 5. Interior view of vaulting and supports of Guell chapel.

4

5

III. RELATIONAL METHODS

I have tried to give the reader some sense of the limits of numerical and analog methods. Though they are rich and valuable for problems in engineering and economics, they are almost useless in designing houses, or any piece of the environment where people are. The reason is simple: no more than a handful of the practical, psychological, and social forces which have the most profound effect on human life can be represented by these methods. Most forces cannot be represented by the variation of any one-dimensional numerical variable. Most forces cannot be represented by "active" forces in an analog.

But there are two valuable lessons to be learned from numerical and analog methods:

1. As all methods of generating form must do, they obtain form from the *interaction* of forces.
2. They succeed in this because they establish a common ground where the forces can interact.

In numerical methods all forces are expressed as numerical variables, and the number system provides the common ground for their interaction. In analog methods all tendencies are expressed as "active" forces, and the physical analog itself is the arena where these active forces can interact.

What we need is a way of allowing a much wider range of tendencies to interact. Bearing this in mind, let me now state the problem once again: *Given a set of forces*, WITH NO RESTRICTION ON THEIR VARIETY, *how can we generate a form which is stable with respect to all of them?*

To solve this problem, we must find a common ground where all forces, of every kind, can interact. This means we must find something which all forces have in common. The only thing that all forces have in common is the fact that each of them is seeking some specific kind of end-state. In more familiar language, each force has certain physical implications. This is the basis of relational methods.[14] There are two key ideas:

1. We try to determine, as abstractly as possible, the physical relation which each individual tendency is seeking.
2. We try to combine these individual abstract relational implications, by fusion, to generate the form.

We may begin to see how the relational implications of forces can be stated, and combined by fusion, in the following example taken from work done several years ago at the Massachusetts Institute of Technology.[15]

The problem was to locate a twenty-mile stretch of highway in Massachusetts, starting from Springfield and ending somewhere near Northampton. We defined twenty-six forces which would influence the location. Each force seeks a certain kind of location for the high-

way. For example, force number 1, the need to reduce earthwork cost, seeks a location through the areas where the land is flat. The full relational implication of each force is represented as a pattern of grays over the terrain: each point in this pattern is dark if the force is likely to generate a highway through that point, and lighter if it is less likely to do so. All twenty-six individual relational implications are shown here. Each corresponds to the entire terrain from Springfield to Northampton.

1. Earthwork Costs

2. Comfort and Safety

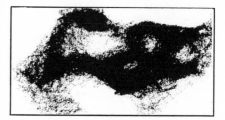

3. Regional Development

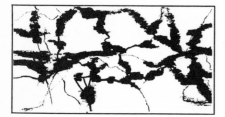

4. Local Land Development

5. Obsolescence

6. Interference During Construction

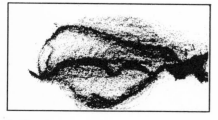

7. User Costs

8. Services

9. Travel Time

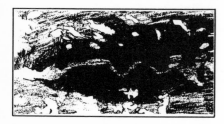

10. Pavement and Subgrade Costs

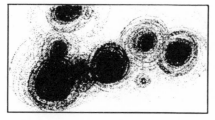

11. Drainage Patterns

12. Bridge Costs

13. Land Costs

14. Eyesores

15. Noise

16. Air Pollution

17. Weather Effects

18. Non-recompensable Public
and Private Losses

19. Public Financial Losses

20. Major Current Traffic Desires

21. Catchment Areas

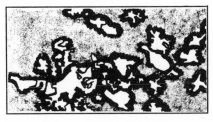

22. Local Accessibility and Integrity

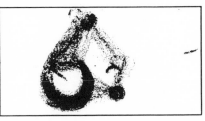

23. Future Transportation Systems

24. Existing Transportation Systems

25. Duplication of Facilities

26. Self-induced Congestion

Fig. 6. Panels 1 through 26 are reproduced from the M. I. T. report, *The Use of Diagrams in Highway Route Location,* by Alexander and Manheim.

Fig. 7.

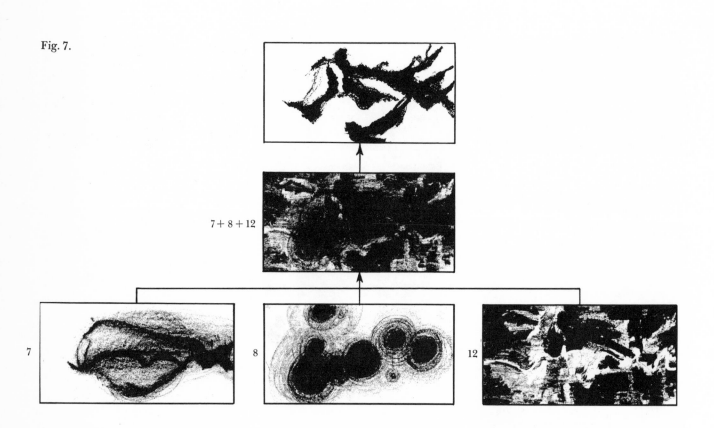

7 + 8 + 12

7   8   12

When two or more of these drawings are super-imposed, a new pattern emerges from the interaction of the individual patterns. This happens because functionally, and visually, the patterns get their meaning from the continuity of density. Two patterns together may form certain continuous strands of darkness, which are not individually present in either of the individual patterns; and in the same way, patterns present in the individual drawings may be submerged in the combination of the two.

Fusion was carried out by superimposing several patterns photographically, and then, from the darkest, most continuous areas in the composite, generating a new pattern (Fig. 7). After a number of processes of fusion, the last fusion generated the pattern A shown in Fig. 8: nothing remains except a pair of lines, one darker than the other. The darkest line defines the best location for the highway (Fig. 9).

This example illustrates the two key ideas of all relational methods. Let me repeat them:

1. We try to determine, as abstractly as possible, the physical relation which each individual force is seeking.
2. We try to combine these individual abstract relational implications, by fusion, to generate the form.

However, the example is unusually simple. First, we know in advance that the highway will be a thin and gently curving line, and this makes the implications easy to state. Second, the underlying terrain provides a constant framework which makes fusion easy. It will usually be much harder to define the implications of individual forces; and much harder to state them in a universal framework, so that they can easily be fused.

Fig. 8.

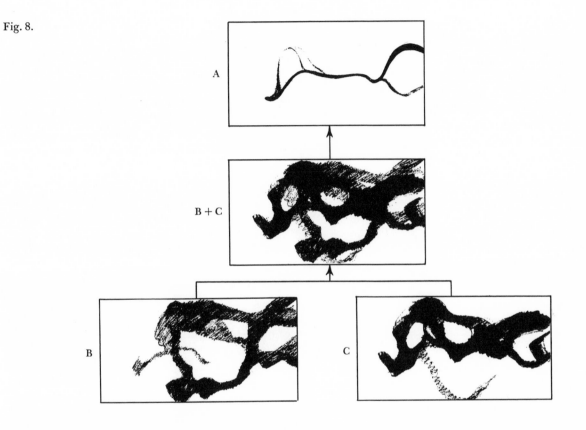

A

B + C

B

C

Fig. 9.

I shall finish by sketching a very simple example which shows these key ideas as they appear in a more general kind of problem. This example deals with the three-way interaction between three forces connected with the "living room" of a house.

I ask the reader to ignore the fact that these three forces are artificially isolated—in a real living room there are perhaps a hundred forces which must all be studied simultaneously. I ask also that he ignore the fact that the abstract relational implications of the individual forces are not clearly expressed; and that he ignore the fact that the process of fusion is not clearly explained. Neither the individual implications nor the fusion can be accurately defined, because at present we still lack any universal way of expressing them.

Lastly, I must ask the reader to remember that, since the example is based on three forces which have been arbitrarily picked out, the form they generate is itself

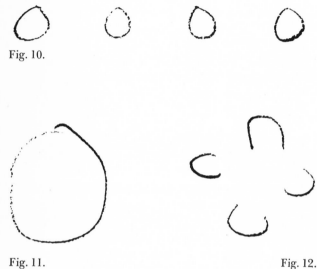

Fig. 10.

Fig. 11.   Fig. 12.

Fig. 13.

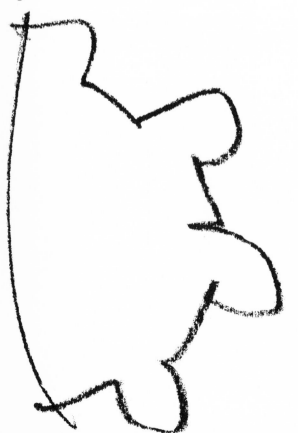

hardly more than a relation: it needs to be fused with many other relations before it actually defines part of a building. The forces are:

1. First of all, each person in a family has his private hobbies: sewing, carpentry, model-building, homework. These activities being what they are, things often need to be left lying about. People therefore tend to do them somewhere where the things can be left lying safely.
2. Second, communal places in a house have to be kept tidy, partly on account of visitors, but also so that no one person's things encroach too heavily on any of the others.
3. Third, there is a tendency for people in the family to want to be together.

Under present circumstances, these three forces are mutually incompatible. The members of the family would like to be together; but in the evenings, and on weekends, when they could be, each one follows up his personal hobbies—sewing, homework, . . . Because these things are messy, and often need to be left standing, people cannot do them in the living room—they would be cleared away too soon. Instead, to do these things each person goes off to his private area—the kitchen, or the basement, or the bedroom—and the family cannot be together.

What are the relational implications of the individual forces?

The first one demands that each person have a private space, where he can do whatever he wants, and where he can leave things, knowing that they will be safe (Fig. 10).

The second one implies that any communal living space, where people come together, must be easy to keep tidy, and people's individual bits and pieces must not encroach on it: hence, that it will be a self-contained spatially integral unit (Fig. 11).

The third implies that when the individual members of the family are following their private interests, they should nevertheless still be with the family as a whole, still be able to see each other, still be within earshot and able to be together easily (Fig. 12).

I have shown these individual relations crudely in the drawings. Fusion of these three relations generates the form shown in the larger drawing (Fig. 13). I shall describe this form concretely, to make it clear. But it must not be interpreted as concrete. It is still an abstract relation—almost certain to be modified by further fusion.

It is a living room with several alcoves in it, one for each person in the family. These alcoves may be left untidy; private bits and pieces are quite safe in them. Each alcove looks into the central living room, and also looks at all the other alcoves. (The angles between alcoves are important.) People in these alcoves can see each other, they can talk to each other, and if they want to they can be together in a moment. Yet, the communal living room itself, because it is a convex whole which excludes the alcoves, is easy to keep tidy. (The alcoves might be fitted with curtains.) The bits and pieces in the individual alcoves do not encroach upon the tidiness of the whole: people can follow their private inclinations and yet be together, simultaneously.

This form, generated by fusion of the relations which each individual force is seeking, is stable with respect to all three forces.

I shall now summarize the argument. The question is: *Given a set of forces,* WITH NO RESTRICTION ON THEIR VARIETY, *how can we generate a form which is stable with respect to them?*

There are very definite limits on numerical and analog methods. It is clear that they cannot cover the full complexity of needs which an environmental problem can contain.

Relational methods, as far as I can see at present, have no such built-in limits. Though the examples I have given are obviously sketchy, relational methods do seem capable of indefinite expansion. They are, in principle, broad enough to deal with all the complexity which an environmental problem can contain. It remains to be seen whether they will be as powerful as they promise.

1. R. G. Hopkinson, *Architectural Physics: Lighting,* London, H.M.S.O. (1963), p. 15.

2. In the thermodynamics of irreversible processes, these tendencies are actually called "forces." S. R. de Groot, *Thermodynamics of Irreversible Processes,* Amsterdam (1961), p. 5.

3. Tyrus Porter, B. Arch. Thesis, Dept. of Architecture (1964), University of California, Berkeley.

4. Theodor Reik, *Of Love and Lust: On the Psychoanalysis of Romantic and Sexual Emotions,* New York (1957), pp. 476–491.

5. R. A. Bagnold, *The Physics of Blown Sand and Desert,* London (1941), pp. 144–153.

6. I have previously called this kind of runaway unaccommodated force a "misfit": *Notes on the Synthesis of Form,* Cambridge, Mass. (1964), Chapter 2.

7. For the problem of assessing forces, see Sim Van der Ryn, *The Ecology of College Housing,* Department of Architecture, University of California, Berkeley, 1965, and forthcoming publications from Barry Poyner and Ian Moore, *Directorate of Development,* Ministry of Works, London, 1966.
See also Henry Murray, "Toward a classification of interactions" in *Toward a General Theory of Action,* (Talcott Parsons and Edward Shils, editors), Cambridge, Mass. (1962), pp. 434–464.

8. For a very simple account, see L. A. Lyusternik, *Shortest Paths,* New York (1964). For a more complete discussion, see Charles Fox, *An Introduction to the Calculus of Variations,* Oxford (1950).

9. Frederick S. Hiller, "*Quantitative Tools for Plant Layout Analysis,*" in *Journal of Industrial Engineering,* vol. 14, no. 1 (Jan.–Feb., 1963), pp. 33–40; Lynn Moseley, "Rational Design Theory," in *Architects Journal,* vol. 11, no. 9 (1963); J. J. Souder *et al., Planning for Hospitals: A Systems Approach Using Computer-aided Techniques,* American Hospital Association, Chicago (1964), pp. 113–162.

10. A. G. M. Michell, "The Limits of Economy of Material in Frame Structures," in *Philadelphia Magazine,* ser. 6, vol. 8 (1904), p. 589. H. L. Cox, *The Design of Structures of Least Weight,* New York (1965), p. 90.

11. W. S. Hemp and H. S. Y. Chan, *Optimum Structures,* College of Aeronautics Memo Areo, no. 70 (July, 1965). The cantilever was designed for the Machine Tool Industry Research Association, Macclesfield, Cheshire.

12. A. G. Shaw, *The Purpose and Practice of Motion Study,* Manchester (1960), pp. 116–120.

13. James Johnson Sweeney and Jose Luis Sert, *Antonio Gaudi,* New York (1960), pp. 74–91.

14. For a very sketchy discussion of the analysis of interacting forces, see *Notes on the Synthesis of Form, op. cit.* Chapters 8, 9, and Appendix 1.

15. Christopher Alexander and Marvin L. Manheim, *The Use of Diagrams in Highway Route Location.* Research Report R62–3, Civil Engineering Systems Laboratory, Massachusetts Institute of Technology (1962). In that report we called the forces "requirements."

LEONARDO RICCI

FORM, THE TANGIBLE EXPRESSION OF A REALITY

The world appears to us. It appears to us above all through a form. The artist expresses himself. He expresses himself through a form. And thus arises the problem: is there an analogy between these "forms"? That is to say, is the form of a man, of a cat, of a stone, analogous to the forms produced by the artist?

I must confess that for some time now I no longer set myself problems of this kind in absolute terms, because I no longer believe in the possibility of "demonstrating" what form is. To be capable of this would mean to be capable of demonstrating what life is. Today, I am interested only in examining how a form is born, that is, how a reality becomes perceivable. Therefore, excluded the possibility of making an abstract contribution, the only possibility which remains to me is that of documenting an experience: my experience in painting and in architecture, my two professions.

FORM IN PAINTING

Anyone faced with the continuous variation in my mode of painting, that is, the variation of my form in painting, must be perplexed. Indeed, I have had periods so diverse that one might think that I have never had a precise concept of form. The truth is otherwise. I believe that my form has been diverse because the contents which this form has expressed have been diverse. Consequently, in opposition to the word *form,* there is the word *content.* We shall see at the end of this paper that these terms will disappear, at least as they have been used up until now.

But why so many and such diverse contents? The answer is simple. Because ever since I was a boy the questions with which life presented me were many, and many were the answers and therefore many the forms. The problem of content and of form is bound to the problem of existence.

To exist means to be born, to live, and to die. Therefore, through my various forms everyone can read all that I have believed and all that I have been in my life. But the process by which form is achieved has always been the same: a reality which found its "form," and not a form conceived a priori.

Now I can answer the question posed at the very beginning of this paper by saying: I do not find a difference in "process" between "natural" form and "artificial" form. The inner reality of the pine tree expresses itself through the form of the pine tree, that of the stone through the form of the stone, and thus that of the cat, thus that of the man. The universe bears its knowledge within itself and expresses itself in form. The honest artist does the same thing.

Today, having found my justification of existence, I believe that I shall not undergo any more earthquakes, either of content or of form.

What do I want to express? And what form is born of this? At this point, since I make notes for each painting, I believe the best thing is to give a documentation of two pictures which were written about as well as painted. It will become more obvious how form is born.

The death of my father: My father died several years ago. I do not even remember the year; perhaps it was nine or ten years ago. My father died in my arms. Death. Man dies. My father died.

What is a dead man in the arms of a living one?

You understand that if I believed in the hereafter, or more precisely, if I were a Christian, this dead body in my arms would be a body waiting for resurrection, for an eternal life. On the other hand, if I believed that nothing exists after death, this body would be only a thing which disintegrates forever in the earth, eaten by maggots.

But my father died and I was neither one nor the other. Facing death, facing my dead father, there was only a son watching the father who slipped away from him, certainly to be forever just as he was then. I could have sworn to nothing in that moment: neither that his soul would rise to heaven, nor that there would be nothing left of him. There was only the subjective recollection of me, his son, of my brothers, his sons, of my mother, who died several years afterwards, perhaps also of a few others.

My father was dead. I was neither desperate nor full of hope. My father was there as I try now to paint him, without bringing in myself and the others.

Before me there is a canvas. Perhaps it is three feet by four feet. Against the brown background of the canvas there is a greenish body: skin and bones, because my father had been ill for three years and he was very thin. A whitish line makes the contour.

It has already been several months since I stopped working on this painting. I did not have the courage to continue it because until this "moment" it was something spontaneous and natural and right "to draw" this body and to detach it slightly from the background by using two different tones. But now I know that it would be unwarranted to add or to take away.

It would be good to set up other canvases. Better still to vary, to change the support, to use wood because I feel more at ease with wood. I shall reproduce this drawing on the new support and try to get something which contains as much as possible of that unknown reality which existed in my presence. Both for me and for the others, because for me it represents my dead father, for the others only a dead man. But what most interests me is death itself.

I draw my father because, having loved him and loving him still in memory, I cannot do so with rhetoric and untruths. My father died in the ordinary bed of a hospital. He died during the night. At two or three o'clock in the morning. My mother, worn out by her vigil which had lasted for days, was sleeping, dressed as she was, in a nearby room.

My father's suffering had lasted for a long time, and for three days, at a sign of his hand or his eyes, I had turned his poor body first to one side, then to the other.

My father died on a white sheet. He was not naked but was covered by some sort of pajama.

Someone could therefore ask if I, by painting him nude and light upon a dark ground, am doing something arbitrary to idealize this death. The question is legitimate. I could ask it myself. The fact is that I remember my father like this, as if he were nude. Perhaps it is because I washed him myself when he was very sick. Perhaps it is because in turning him I felt neither sheet nor pajama but only the suffering body. Besides, when today I approximate as closely as possible that which I saw and lived through, I still do not know exactly what color my father's body will assume, nor that of the color of the plane on which it rests. Because color does not make sense unless it signifies a specific thing in a specific circumstance. Color by itself has no meaning other than as a decorative thing. Here it is a question of using form and color which express real things.

Much time has passed: three, four, ten months, I don't remember. That I don't is due to the fact that for me the days have again become long, as when I was a boy. They are no longer harried and fleeting. The day once again belongs to time.

Now there are two paintings instead of one. The difference between the two is that in the first there is only the recollection of my dead father; the second is my father, but dead for everyone, dead even for others: a dead man.

Perhaps the painting is finished. Certainly this dead man is different from those previously painted, at least it seems so to me. There is no fear of death in it, nor hope of a paradise, nor affirmation of what is death. There is only that mystery which death carries with it. That expression of reality which the death of a man produces. That sense of expectation—no matter what expectation. That interruption of an unknown rhythm, that of life, to become part of another unknown, that of death.

That body will no longer breathe. It will no longer speak to me. It will no longer smile at me. All that there was of life is finished forever.

But that body is there to testify to a real contact which took place between me and my father when he was at the point of death, exactly at the moment when life "left" him. When everything, apparently absurd and without reason, silently testified to an inner logic such as I had never felt before. So much so that I can say that never in my life did I understand myself to be so bound by the vicissitudes of man, and not only of man but of the earth and of the whole universe. That is to say, I was thrust into the world without knowing why, nor caring why, and the more I became a part of it, the less I could detach myself to ask the question.

That dead body. So like all those already dead, those who at this moment are dying, those who will die.

My wife in childbirth: More exactly, my wife in the night which followed her giving birth, which had occurred at one o'clock in the morning, with the baby—or rather, the baby girl—beside her.

My wife gave birth in my house. She was asleep in the same room. She slept in the big bed, I in a little bed at her feet. It was night but there was some light in the room. I am in the habit of leaving the windows uncovered because I love the light which the night gives. My wife and daughter slept. I heard two breaths in the room: that tired, and slow, and strong of my wife and that rapid, scarcely perceptible of my daughter. I did not hear my own. At least I was not aware of it. From time to time I got up to look at those two creatures in their sleep.

The picture which I am drawing and which already begins to take form, wants to be a testimonial to that night. The two bodies are nude while that night they were hidden in part by the covers. But I saw only their bodies and I remember that my wife's hair, a chestnut-blond color, became so black in the nocturnal light that the visual focus was her pale face surrounded by the shadow of her hair. I watched them for a long time, attentive to each small movement, waiting for their call. A kind of adoration of my wife and of my daughter and of the miracle of maternity.

There are moments during the execution of a painting in which one shows the force and the character of he who is painting. These are the moments of transition in which a thing of "imagination" becomes "concrete."

I find myself in one of these moments. The night, the presence of the mother in the night, the child who has not yet achieved a precise form, her pretty little face still shows signs of birth, of a difficult birth. All these things are present on the wood. I could stop. It is all evanescent and full of wonder. But I remember how, despite the night, I saw the form clearly. Even the sunlight could not have defined it more sharply, such was the attention and the quietness and the care with which I observed each small detail. So that the image was strikingly exact, even in those things which the eye could not see. I was so very aware of that belly which earlier that day I had pressed with all my strength and hurt, because at the very moment of giving birth the mother's strength had died out and the baby, later my daughter, risked death with her little head suspended halfway, at the threshold between going out into life and remaining in the warmth of her mother's belly. Thus this belly swollen with the wound, and the blood, and those things inside a woman, placenta, umbilical cord, water, which were still present—even though it was now all over—present at least in me there observing these creatures asleep.

Certainly this is the moment of danger. I can ruin the picture. But I am fortunate. The picture in itself does not interest me. What does matter is to see if I am capable of defining that state of my existence and theirs. I want whoever looks at it to feel that I am not outside the rectangle of wood, even if I am not visible.

The mistake. Certainly the mistake. Better to make it evident, if it exists. Not to conceal it within the picture.

After two days of hard work the painting is all black again. I want to explain the reason, that is to say, the "moments" of this painting. There was a first phase during which the painting was extremely pictorial but lacked reality. Then I wanted to define the contour with more exactness and strength. I cut into the wood with a pyrographic instrument. With the fire I felt that I could render the strength which maternity has. But the needles were small and the incision in the wood superficial. The fire gave strength, but the painting became brutal, whereas in the night I had felt strength, yes, but pervaded with a sweetness which the fire killed.

So this morning I repainted the picture with oil colors. Slow overlays of color. But the figures became slimy, "varnished," a little like all those oil paintings, even those by painters like Raphael or Titian. Beneath the "film" there is nothing. A theatrical pretense. That pretense which good sculptures —like some of those of Giovanni Pisano in the Baptistry at Pisa—often do not have, because the material remains material. But in a painting the problem changes, because the problem of the material changes. However much I try to enrich the nature of the material, the wood always remains without depth. The mistake in the painting. Because beneath the real skin there is blood and flesh and the brain and the heart. Beneath the skin of the painting there is nothing. And this is the tragedy: the feelings of the painter, who has seen and understood, are more tangible than the object itself, which is not really seen and understood, yet is real.

When I was a "painter" I would have been upset enough to die over this human impotence. Today no. I wait for something to happen, trying to understand what it is that passes between the real object and the represented one, what there is in the represented object, and how it can render that truth which the real object has but which flees from the inattentive observer.

For the present the painting is only a dirty, black thing, but it has mystery.

While I wait for the glues and oils of the painting to dry, I try to think which among the maternities represented in painting and sculpture have struck me most and which seem to me nearest to what I should like to express.

The sculptures. Above all, some in wood by African sculptors. Some Mexican ones in terra cotta. Some Indian ones in stone. Certainly wood—especially when time has removed its polished external skin, and revealed the antiquity of its fibers, that sense of the sap which has run through it for years, its organic strength, even if now spent—has helped the artist in his expression. But the phallic content and the endogenous forces of the mother are so strong that they obscure those other things one might see in a maternity, such as the subtle relationship which exists between a smile and the miracle. A miracle because it is so little understood and is, at least until now, impossible to achieve in the laboratory. For even those acts which precede maternity, and all those of maternity itself, are not important in themselves but for the fact that they bring man back to possibilities once considered to be of a metaphysical and spiritual order. Possibilities which today are not definable, but are certainly bound to that reality which pervades all things and makes life beautiful.

But as I think of those wooden sculptures, where is the awareness outside that of the event itself, that consciousness of the two people breathing, for example, and the presence of myself in that room, of myself as I was watching?

How to realize and represent the reality of my own presence in that maternity, I who did not see myself with my own eyes, but who nevertheless existed?

What could make my presence tangible without translating it into surrealistic and expressionistic terms? How to materialize the outline of myself which no one saw? That is, how to place myself within the space of this painting?

In this instance, as before, a certain amount of time has passed. I should have liked to have reported carefully all the "relations" between me and the painting that changed as the painting proceeded. More precisely, all the events that took place between me and the reality of that night.

Now I consider the painting finished. Not because I was able to achieve a perfect identity between myself today and myself that night. On the contrary, I feel that an infinite number of elements have escaped me and are not attested to. I consider it finished only because there is nothing arbitrary. Nothing that creates a false charm. Nothing which puts the observer before an insoluble problem. Many things are missing. But that which is there is enough for me to bear witness to a birth.

In the night the mother was alive and alive was the daughter. In the night the mother breathed and so breathed the daughter. In the night mother and daughter were bound by the umbilical cord which binds us all together in this terrestrial adventure. But in the painting all that is not possible and will never be possible. The painting will only serve as a remembrance, to focus more attention on what birth means. Because the whole secret of existence is only to know how to seize at each moment the marvelous possibility of existence.

FORM IN ARCHITECTURE

Whoever follows my work as an architect will note fewer alternatives and changes than in my painting. The development of form here has a more regular and continuous progress. There are definite reasons for this. First of all because I began to design and build later. At twenty-six rather than at fourteen. At a more mature age. Besides, architecture is bound to more limited themes because it must solve problems which have not been chosen by the architect. Moreover, the logic of construction impedes gratuitous freedom of form. Finally, when I was in a state of crisis, I did not design. However, from a formal point of view, an evolution has occurred which I might express in these terms: architectural form has increasingly freed itself from theoretical presuppositions to be united with its content, that is, to be born from its content.

If the content of a picture seems more obvious to some, given that the rapport between the painter and the canvas is immediate, while the rapport between the architect and the building is modified by many components (client, cost, function, structure), this does not mean that architecture does not have content. The process of achieving form is not different from that of painting. I shall illustrate this, as I did for painting.

The birth of my house: I wanted to build a house for myself. More or less like everyone else, my wife and I set out to find some land which would be suitable for us. And since we no longer wanted to live in the old central part of the city, because it no longer suited us, we looked for some land on a hill. But not, for example, Fiesole, or Bellosguardo, which still have a feeling of the old city. Rather, we looked for a virgin hill and especially one in a place where the vegetation was natural, not planted by man: broom and thicket on a rocky terrain.

We chose a place which, although it was without gentleness and humanity, permitted us to experiment with a new way of living, in regard to the relationship between a man and his own house.

The variety of a house and the process to the final form of a building can come about in a thousand ways. I shall describe mine.

My wife and I did not reason this way, for example: that we needed so many bedrooms, a living room, a kitchen, two baths, etc. We started from something different. We asked ourselves what it meant to awaken. How we would wish to open ourselves to the world each morning, to the life of a day. We asked ourselves what it meant to go to sleep, that is, to close our day. What it meant to eat, to be among ourselves or with friends. How to give the children their own private place to develop their own natures, and also a collective place so that they would learn to be with others, even if for now only among themselves.

In short, I did not seek to put a beautiful dress on conformist and a priori-accepted functions, but on the contrary, to examine the acts of our own daily life in order to make them, through their contact with the architecture, more vital, more important. The act and then the consequent form. That is to say, I saw us getting up in the morning, my wife and myself and our children; I saw her go to get them ready for school; I saw the children chatting with their friends, we with ours, our being and living together and with others, our entering the house and leaving it to go into the countryside. And not only these things, which seem beautiful and poetic. I also saw the milkman bringing the milk, the vegetable vender the vegetables. That is to say, I tried to see our life in all its aspects.

So the space was born to contain us. The structure to materialize that space. The form is a consequence of all this. The reasons for the form, that is to say, are not born from aesthetic or hedonistic preoccupations.

A floor was put at a certain height to suspend us in the void. A wall was erected to protect us from the wind. Another to relate the hills in front with the center of the house. A material to give concreteness to the force of gravity. "Style" was destroyed, and the form was not intellectual or conceptual. It was simply born.

For eleven years now we have lived there. We have not been bored; it has not grown old. It lives with us as a dog or a cat might, or better, a beloved person.

I have used my house as an example because for me it is the simplest, most familiar thing. But I could make the same kind of analysis for each type of structure. The problem is the same. It is a question of establishing whether the architect chooses his form or whether he is forced to his form by necessity. I believe that the falseness and gratuitousness of the first attitude and the truth of the second are obvious. Arriving at an apparent paradox, I might say that the architect has absolutely no choice.

At the basis of the actual design various components exist: the client, the available funds, the land on which the building will rise, the environment, the system of construction, the materials. Then there is the architect, the architect with his own reality, with his personality, with his biology.

The more precise the analysis of all these elements, the more the architect will find himself in a position of not being able to choose. Faced with the reality of the starting-point, the architect can only make these realities achieve their own nature and translate them into form. Not a dictator, therefore, but a servant, that is to say, in the service of man.

Someone might ask me: But poetry? But imagination? But beauty? What are these? I could answer that I do not believe any more in poetry, in imagination, in beauty. But I do not wish to be equivocal. I say: A flower, does it not perhaps contain poetry, imagination, beauty? And perhaps does not the marvelous face of a woman? Is not the poetry, the imagination, the beauty of a flower or the face of a woman the result of the reality intrinsic to the flower or to the woman? And why must it be different in architecture? Is man, in this case the architect, perhaps something different, detached from the internal logic of the world? Can the architect detach himself from this internal logic? And if the architect acts strictly in accordance with the content that is given him, is his architecture then perhaps nothing other than the product of this internal light?

I could continue at length about architecture. As for painting, I have examined the birth of two pictures, I could for architecture examine other of my designs: house, store, or factory. As I could also examine still others which I have not yet had the fortune to design: schools, hospitals, skyscraper offices. But even for these the analysis would not be different. Instead of the life of my family, I would examine the lives of children, of sick people, of clerks. I would examine the acts which they perform or which they will perform, these future inhabitants of future organisms. From these acts form arises naturally.

Thus, in architecture as in painting, form is only a result. In painting it arises as testimony to acts which have happened or which are happening; in architecture as the presence of acts which have happened or which are happening.

In conclusion I must say that for me form no longer presents itself as a problem. The contents that produce form no longer present themselves as problems. So that it is basically absurd to speak of content, and perhaps the very word "form" becomes so inappropriate as a semantic extension of the concept as to destroy the word form as a concept. In other words, I am fed up with all the intellectualisms and with all the preoccupations which are aesthetic or pseudo-aesthetic, literary or pseudo-literary, ethical or pseudo-ethical, in art and in form. And I say to myself, returning to the first question which was posed as a problem and is now no longer a problem: The form of the cat is born because inside there is the cat, the form of the mountain because inside there is the mountain, that of the woman because inside there is the woman. The form of a house because inside there is that house. That of a painting because inside there is that painting.

I have said "inside" to make it understood that form is nothing but the visual experience of an internal reality. But even this word "inside" can become equivocal because it might seem that there is an inside and therefore an outside, thus a content and a form, but in reality one should not even speak of an inside.

Form is nothing other than the tangible expression of a reality and when this truly coincides with reality it is in consequence true, it is in consequence beautiful.

On the following pages are three models, examples of the research for a "Not Alienated" urbanism presently being carried on by Leonardo Ricci, and his assistants and students at the University of Florence. The different forms of these models are the natural result of the different conceptions for the three structures, but they are all based on the same hypotheses for a "Not Alienated" town.

Organism studied in reinforced concrete. Megastructure in
extruded pylons, with different types of beams according to
specific needs. In the megastructure can be integrated at
different times not only the communication system, but also
secondary structures containing organisms of diverse functions.

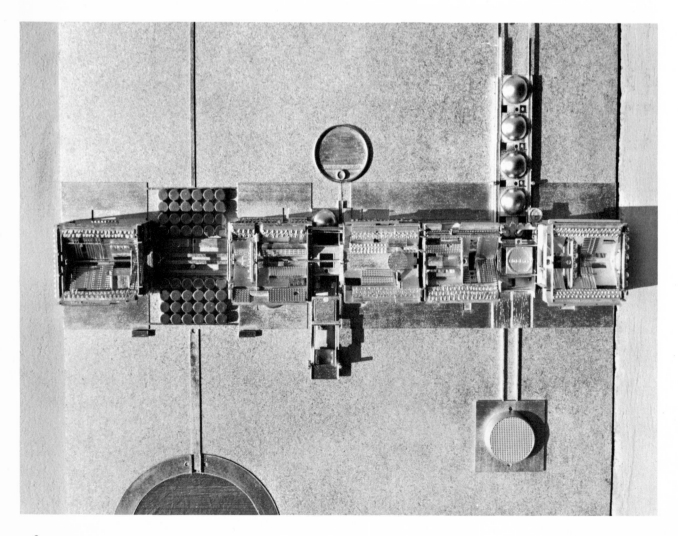

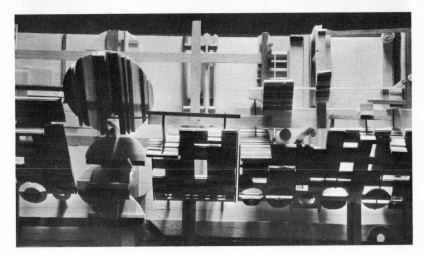

MODEL II

Continuous organism which combines different industrialized structures and space according to their various needs and functions. The organism can grow in any direction and at any time.

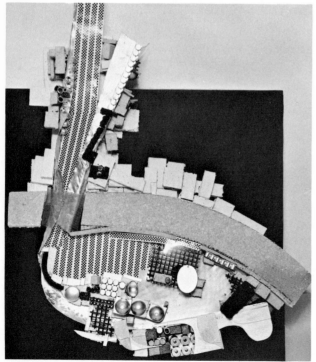

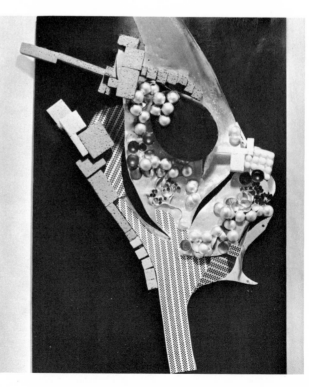

MODEL III

Continuous organism constructed in a plastic material which
permits the growth of space for different uses.

Probably the most decisive factor in the forming of a building is its visible structure, the interplay of supported and supporting parts—a materialization of stresses working in dead matter.

Construction is indeed a very old human activity, fired and driven not only by practical requirements, but by instincts. We may justly call these instincts atavistic. To have a roof over us is not merely a protection from sun and rain, but an instinctive need: small children like to play under a chair, a table, under a roof of their own, though they are already protected by the roof of the house. The child, nearly every child, starts to construct without need or purpose.

To defeat gravity, to lift and move and support weight, to rise high up and then higher, may be regarded instinctive and atavistic too. The history of construction outlines our struggle with the material, with its weight, with gravity—from the prehistoric pile of rock and the tree house, to the span of the Golden Gate Bridge, and to the swaying frame of the Eiffel Tower. We may rationalize about the drive against gravity: the Tower of Babel may establish communication with God, the rocket may serve research concerning the moon, the satellite may provide an observation point, and the skyscraper may exploit or create land values. Whatever our excuse, the domination of height, the direction away from gravity, the lifting and floating of heavy matter remain part of the human record.

The conception of enclosures for our daily needs, for living and working, for the intricate complex of requirements, determines to a certain degree the size and shape of our buildings and to a greater degree the interior spaces defined by the building.

At the beginning of the design process, all is a bodiless assemblage in the abstract—weights are without support, walls without thickness: a mere diagram of the needs.

As we develop the design, we inevitably arrive at the point where the problem "what to build" expands into the problem "how to build." The theoretical, lineal enclosure of space then receives the thickness of a wall, of a slab, of a column, of components made of material having mass, weight, and shape. The abstract process of planning changes over into the tangible science of construction. The necessity for a certain kind of space now becomes intrinsically connected with the art of building. The lineal sketch, the plan and the purpose of our diagram grows into weight and mass and form. The aspect of material enters the design process, with its laws and sympathies and details: Architecture.

The analytical approach, investigating the purpose first, developing the basic needs in an abstract, lineal diagram, nursing this composition of sequences and dimensions into a physical structure, using the conflicts between demands and the experienced nature of materials as inspiration for architectural three-dimensional buildings, spaces, masses, and voids—this approach is the achievement of the twentieth century. That most needed working diagram in the abstract was perhaps a major fascination of our new architecture, and to come as close to it as possible resulted in the utmost transparency of the building, in the lineal façade, weightless, a mere reflection—with little relation to material, to mass. With little relation also to the human material, to our need for things to touch, to lean against, to cover.

The vocabulary of architecture expands: solids, three-dimensional masses, plasticity, appear next to transparent elements; form appears next to pure proportions: the depth of the façade—sun and shadow. The abstract space does not claim universality. It claims to be truer in its variations and adaptations to our varied needs, to differentiations of visible structural solutions, to our three-dimensional, human instincts.

Fig. 1. Research Center for IBM, La Gaude, France, 1960.
Marcel Breuer, architect; Robert F. Gatje, associate;
Richard Laugier and Michel Laugier, supervising architects.

Figs. 2 and 3. First idea sketch and final plan for Ustinov
House, Vevey, Switzerland, 1959. Marcel Breuer, architect;
Robert F. Gatje, associate. The design is a cluster plan of four
units—living, parents, children, guests—connected with patios
and terraces.

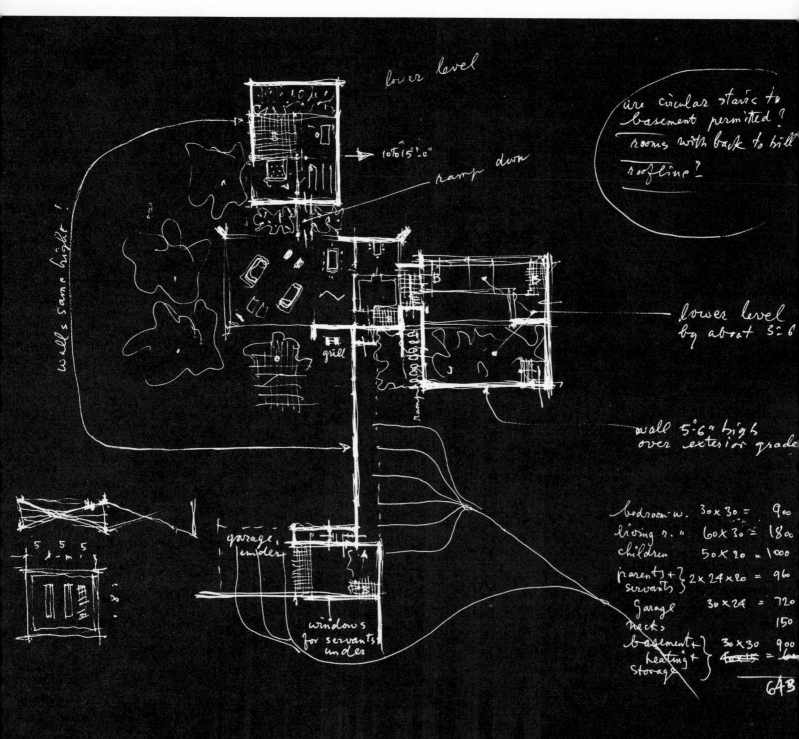

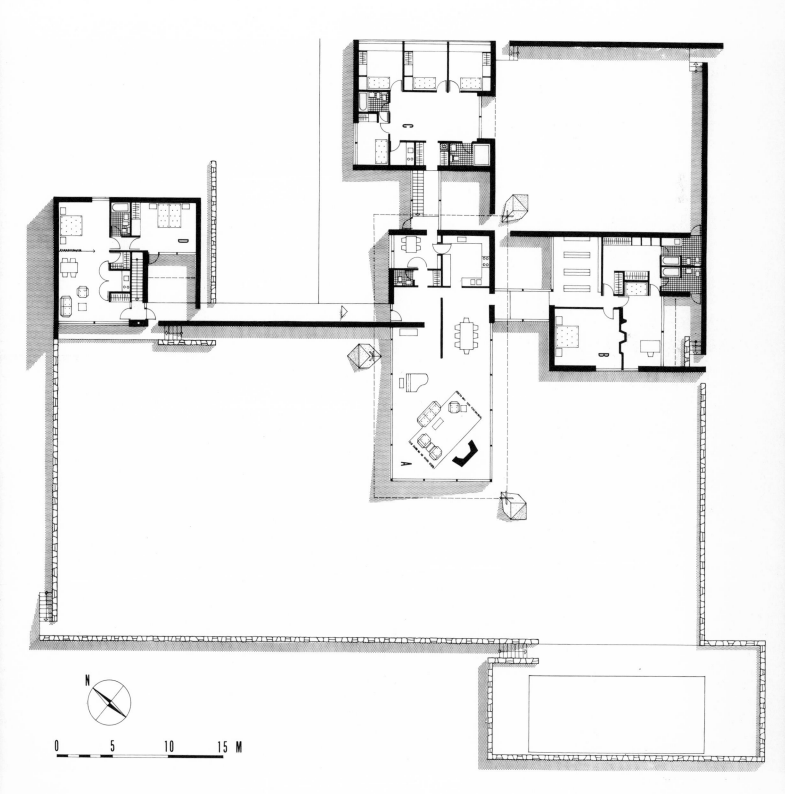

N

0   5   10   15 M

Fig. 4. Research Center for IBM, La Gaude, France, 1960. View showing stone base of entry ramp and curvature of façade. Marcel Breuer, architect; Robert F. Gatje, associate; Richard Laugier and Michel Laugier, supervising architects.

Fig. 5. St. John's Abbey Church, Collegeville, Minnesota, 1953–1961.
View of bell banner and stained-glass and concrete hexagonal
wall. Marcel Breuer, architect; Hamilton Smith, associate.

THEODORE M. BROWN

RIETVELD AND THE MAN-MADE OBJECT

Only within such a fertile ferment as the World War I period could a man like Gerrit Thomas Rietveld● enter international architecture and contribute to a collective design consciousness. A self-taught cabinetmaker whose vision developed in shortsighted Utrecht, he appeared on the European artistic scene around 1918 with his now famous Red-Blue chair, recognized and publicized by the farsighted *de Stijl* group.

Conceived as though he had never seen a chair, Rietveld established planes for horizontal and vertical support and a skeletal frame to suspend them, a pristine space composition of classical pedigree. This "slender space animal," as Theo van Doesburg characterized it, was the germ of Rietveld's own architecture; and the composition entered the pool of European design at the beginning of the 1920's.

Around 1921 Rietveld designed a jewelry shop (since destroyed) in Amsterdam. Glazed, discontinuous, rectilinear volumes, perpendicularly related, linked the inside with the outside in a space continuum channeled by discrete, colored surfaces. This was the first full-scale architectural application of *de Stijl* principles, then being formulated.

Constructed in 1924, the well known Schröder house in Utrecht, designed in collaboration with its owner, Truus Schröder-Schräder, marks the swift culmination of Rietveld's mastery of a fresh design vocabulary. Similar to its furniture progenitor, volumes are defined by independent, interlocking planes. Like the interior of traditional Japanese houses, the open space of the upper level can be subdivided by sliding panels. The lower level is composed of small, interlocking space cubicles. Planes, as though suspended by hidden magnets, seem forever shifting their relationships as observer moves in and around the building. Clashing with its archaic surroundings, the house was an uncompromising manifesto of the pristine *new* within the decaying *old,* an architectural phoenix rising proudly from the ashes of

prewar Europe, and has remained a fountain of youth, joy, and hope, even within our own world of escalating psychic and physical traumas.

The insectile table lamp (1925), glazed radio cabinet (1925), and garage-living quarters (1927–28) are but a few more of the myriad of small objects issued from his fertile mind. The reality of the lamp—its "lampness"— is forcefully expressed by the bare, half-painted bulb, primly poised upon its metallic stalk. The visual satisfaction of electronic components has never been more candidly promoted than in Rietveld's radio cabinet, a whiff of the future. And the garage, constructed of prefabricated concrete planes suspended within a modular metallic frame, manifests a fresh approach to the problem of industrialized architecture.

During the next decade (1928–1938) the visual gains of the early Twenties were consolidated and applied; but here Rietveld's elemental vision was not as relevant as it was during the period when a formal syntax was being established. Yet, after World War II he recaptured the flair that characterized his early, historically pregnant, works. The sculpture pavilion at Arnhem (destroyed; rebuilt recently in the garden of the Kröller-Müller Museum, Otterlo), the Van der Doel and Van Slobbe houses, all built during the last decade of his life, exhibit the old wizardry, now combined with an assurance accrued with time.

Throughout his life Rietveld's work and thought exhibit a stubborn single-mindedness rare in our frenetic world. His lifetime concentration on the designed object parallels the patient pursuit of an artistic ideal by other Dutchmen such as Vermeer and Mondrian. Rare also is Rietveld's intellectual position, which bears little relation to the prevalent aesthetic and technical ideals of contemporary architects.

We construct objects for a variety of reasons: utilitarian, military, aesthetic; things are made also to record experience and to embody values. Rietveld built

●

Born 1888 in Utrecht, The Netherlands; worked as cabinetmaker until 1919 when he became an independent architect and joined *de Stijl;* founding member of C.I.A.M. in 1928; and practicing architect until his death in Utrecht, 1964. See T. M. Brown, *Work of G. Rietveld, Architect,* Utrecht, 1958.

Fig. 1. Red-Blue chair, about 1918. Photo Hulskamp.

2

3

2a

Fig. 2. Baby chair, about 1920.

Fig. 2a. Structural detail of same chair.

Fig. 3. Baby chair, about 1919.

Fig. 4. Chair, 1919.

Fig. 5. Berlin chair, 1923.

Fig. 6. Zig-zag chair, 1934.

for still another reason. "The purpose of art," he said, "is to develop and nourish a specific sense organ." •

As our senses are more or less cultivated, we become more or less aware, and our consciousness develops. Breadth of vision depends upon growth of awareness. *Welfare of our being depends upon the development and health of the senses.*

With reverence for "the immediate life, the ordinary, simple, direct experience of reality," Rietveld formulated his goal: intensification of life-enhancing sensory experience. His method: cumulative visual experience, catalyzed by the designed object.

Assuming that "All . . . experience is based upon the activity of our senses," Rietveld wrote that "the absorption and digestion of sensory information" develops ourselves, awareness of surroundings, and our grasp of reality. "The process of becoming conscious [*bewustwording*] of reality determines both our nature and our image of environment."

Rietveld's reality is restricted to that conscious awareness of the visible world gained through sensory activity. As he explained:

If I looked at something, for example, a newspaper clipping, I saw dots [and] understood that I was not supposed to see them; because there is a definite scale whereby I should see the paper. With a magnifying glass I saw only different dots without any image; and had I looked through a microscope I would have seen fibers, threads, and specks. I knew that I was supposed to see a newspaper, letters, and an image; and I determined for myself the scale necessary for this experience. Such a scale is obvious for the newspaper; but there are things and ideas where the scale is not so easily determined and can be observed only through proper scale. And there are many realities; and different creatures have special sensory systems [to experience these realities]. What then is reality . . . ?
[Rietveld's conclusion:] . . . reality is that experience which is circumscribed by our humanly scaled percepts to see, hear, and taste.

Yet, since "Sensory activity is very limited and varies from person to person," awareness is inherently nar-

•

All quotations are from Rietveld. For a more comprehensive analysis of Rietveld's theoretical position, see T. M. Brown, "Rietveld's Egocentric Vision," in *Journal of the Society of Architectural Historians,* vol. 24 (1965), pp. 292–296.

rowly restricted; because only a small fraction of external stimuli penetrates our selective sensory apparatus. We peek out at the world through the slightly open doors of our restricted human systems; and with the data which filters through the screen of unaided senses, we establish the outer world for ourselves in accordance with the specialized nature of our system, thus creating our reality.

This reality develops gradually in correspondence with the awakening of our consciousness. Step by step we gain meaningful awareness of our surroundings: a single, finite world-image [*wereldbeeld*].
Through our own existence we feel partnership with cosmic events; the growth of our consciousness *to be* enlarges with the urge to be a part of general life . . .
Our *Umwelt* and our *I* grow each time a snapshot of life is absorbed by our consciousness.
Growth = joy.

Art, according to Rietveld, is an activity which identifies, clarifies, and intensifies reality; each of the visual arts must specialize in a different aspect of reality; painting for color; sculpture for form; architecture for space. Each requires a special vision; and the artist's job is to

Fig. 7. Lamp, 1920.

Fig. 8. Buffet, 1919.

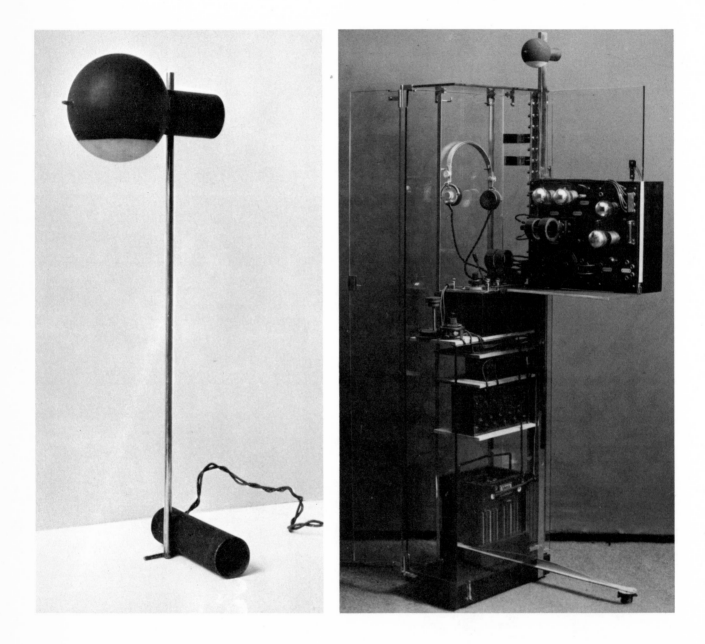

Fig. 9. Table lamp, 1925.

Fig. 10. Radio cabinet, 1925.

formulate his particular material so as to maximize experience within his specific sphere.

Through an art object we enter joyfully into a piece of reality, in contrast to the perceptions which we usually undergo passively . . . From what height or depth came the spark of consciousness we do not know; but certainly we experience joy through growth and melancholy through withdrawal of our being. Every passive sensation shrinks us . . .

Every art work contributes something to the activity of the senses, not because the artist is greater than others; but, through his specialized application of the senses, the artist concentrates on only one aspect of nature.

Where some artists view limitations as life-crippling, Rietveld rejoiced in them; because

. . . limitations of seeing are necessary, [as] unlimited space is not visible (and actually does not exist). The spatial value of a tower is that it defines place and measures height, thus making the space around it "real."

Unreflected light does not illuminate space. Material is visible only through its limitation, the separation of material and environment; [and] environment becomes color only through a limited color surface.

Paraphrasing Rabindranath Tagore, as he did frequently in his writing, Rietveld wrote:

Tagore says, speaking about the nature of art: Through limitation of the unlimited, truth becomes real. Every art work illuminates a facet of the reality of the observer and gives us the joy of creating the basis of our existence.

Art in general, architecture in particular, is not concerned primarily with beauty but with the clear expression of the appearance of form . . . Tagore says: "Art has no other objective than that it appears to be be" [Rietveld added,] what it is.

Art should become detached from its creator; and indeed it "will destroy itself; only a great artist can create pure artless work."

Art is not a luxurious excess or, even worse, a kind of spiritual sublimity which stands outside, above, or beside society. . . . art is action.

Art is not a matter of liking . . . [and] is *certainly not concerned with the making of beauty;* it has no transcendental objective or tendency. The purpose of art is to develop and nourish a definite sense organ. It is the one-sided, yet immediate, experience of reality, the ordinary, simple experience for which we need only open the eyes or extend the hand.

Perception of an art work is not contingent upon impetuosity of brushstroke; virtuosity of line; or the dramatic, comic, or epic quality of its subject. It depends only on its clarity. We can absorb space, color, and material only through their clear limitation.

Through appearance of form, color, sound, odor, and . . . hardness [a] thing becomes real (perceptible) for us. That we find this reality beautiful or ugly is a question of relationship and insight, in each case a personal preference or aversion.

Art clarifies reality and carries personal beauty to a general form language.

As a cabinetmaker turned architect, Rietveld's principal media were material and space; and in his view, *"the reality which architecture can create is space,"* the most fundamental reality of all.

Space is the first discovery of man; through separation of *I* and *environment* there originates a sense of *becoming conscious [bewustwording]*, what for convenience we call consciousness.

The first step toward consciousness is the knowledge of an individual existence, and this begins with the separation of the *I* and the space around the *I*. One can observe this in a growing baby. *Therefore space means more than other elements as a necessity of life.*

For selfish reasons we must love our environment and our neighbor as our self. And architecture is the best profession constituted to realize the spatial expansion of our *I* and to create a livable human scale; because the medium of architecture is space.

Characteristic of all architecture is that we live in it, on it, around it, and between it.

Art forces the activity of one, or a part, of our senses; for architecture it is our space sense. Isolated fragments of primary reality enlighten our consciousness, through clarification of our discernment. They *provide* and *maintain* our joy of living, which then becomes less dependent on "having," on property and power.

[This "primary reality"] broadens the scale of our *wereldbeeld.*

Explaining the space-defining nature of his early furniture, Rietveld said in 1919:

With this chair an attempt has been made to have every part simple and in its most elementary form in accordance with function and material, thus the form which is most capable of being harmonized with the whole. The construction is attuned to the parts to insure that no part dominates or is subordinate to the others. In this way, the whole stands freely and clearly in space, and form stands out from material.

The wood connection used here is obvious because of its

simplicity and clarity of expression . . . the greatest advantage [of the system] is that one is very free in placing the rails, thus giving the object a greater spatial expression, which liberates one from the constructive-bound plane.

As an instrument in the process of realization, architecture establishes tentative conditions which bring life to an ever richer fulfillment.

Life as a whole is like a balance eternally seeking its center of gravity, . . . the practice of architecture is a sober self-maintenance . . . [Therefore] we must not consider the human scale, which in our field is so highly praised, as a cultural attainment. Because . . . we must bring things into a human scale, in contrast with the inhuman in nature, as a means of self-preservation.

. . . I see architecture more as a tenuous equilibrium than as an unshakable monumentality!

Each work is only a part of the unending expressional possibilities; and an attempt toward completeness in a single work would injure the harmony.

Man's goal is "to realize one's existence, to discern the self from that which is outside oneself and to awaken one's consciousness." This is accomplished through the medium of the human body, assisted by the man-made object, resulting in a "direct experience of reality." Thus,

All perceptions and experiences unite in knowing; and all alter our condition, either toward joy (expansion) or melancholy (contraction) . . .

Architecture is not a matter of beauty or ugliness, but of clarity . . .

Good architecture is a fragment of reality which forces a partial expansion of our self . . . It is the background of our life, neither more beautiful nor ugly; but if it is good: clear . . .

Fig. 11. Garage-living quarters, Utrecht, 1927–1928.

Fig. 12. Van Slobbe House, Heerlen, 1961–1964.

Fig. 13. Van der Doel House, Ilpendam, 1958–1959.

OBJECT-DESIGN: SIGNIFICANT EXAMPLES

Marcel Breuer: Furniture designed
in bent continuous tubular steel.
Fig. 1. Wassily chair, 1925.
Fig. 2. Cantilever chair, 1928.
Fig. 3. Glass-top table with tubular
steel frame, 1928.
Fig. 4. Folding "Director's chair," 1928.

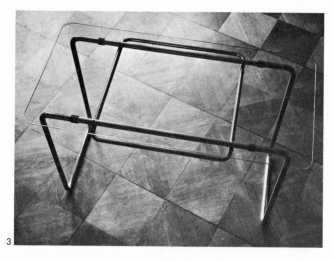

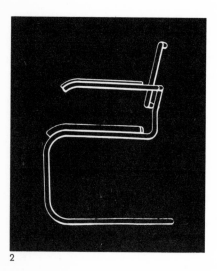

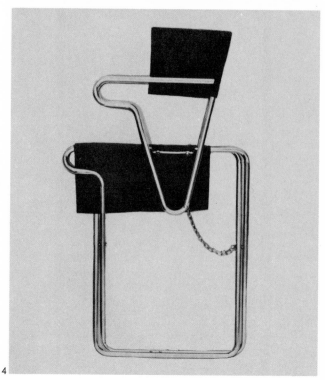

Marcel Breuer: Furniture designed in plywood.
Fig. 5. Isokon reclining chair
and coffee table, 1935.
Fig. 6. Table, 1935.
Fig. 7. Cut-out plywood nesting chair, 1948.

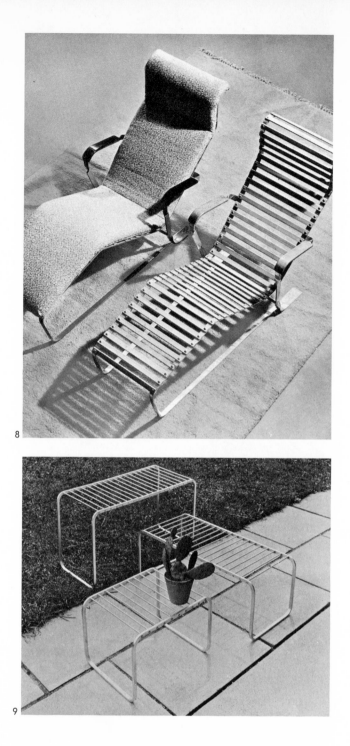

8

9

Marcel Breuer: Furniture designed in aluminum.
Fig. 8. Chaise-longue.
Fig. 9. Stools or occasional tables.

10

11

Marcel Breuer: Furniture designed for nesting.
Fig. 10. Pattern of nesting parts for cut-out plywood chair, 1948.
Fig. 11. Five plywood nesting chairs, 1935.

Marcel Breuer: Designs for a community of objects.
Fig. 12. Living room, Thoost House, Hamburg, 1926.
Fig. 13. Dining room, Piscator Apartment, Berlin, 1927.

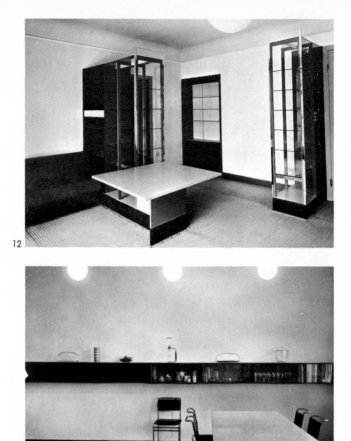

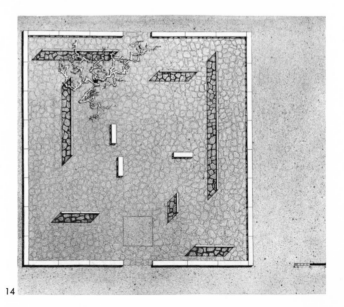

Fig. 14. Project for a Servicemen's Memorial, Cambridge, Massachusetts, 1945. Designed in association with Lawrence Anderson. 70' x 70' paved area bisected by the center path of Cambridge Common, and defined by peripheral cast-stone benches. Translucent glass panels, cantilevered from the ground, bear names of 16,000 World War II servicemen.

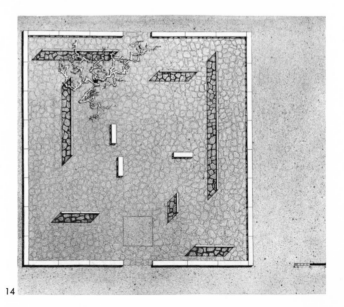

Fig. 15. Marcel Breuer in partnership with
F.R.S. Yorke, "Civic Center of the Future,"
1936. Close-up view of exhibition model for
British Cement and Concrete Association.

16

17

Fig. 16. Alvar Aalto. Upholstered chair with laminated spring arms, 1929–1930.

Fig. 17. Alvar Aalto. Low backed side chair with padded seat, and high-backed side chair with plywood seat.

Fig. 18. Ludwig Mies van der Rohe. Dining chair of tubular steel and hide.

Fig. 19. Ludwig Mies van der Rohe. Side chairs of chromium-plated steel and leather covering. Photos courtesy Knoll Associates, Inc.

18

19

143

21

Ludwig Mies van der Rohe.

Fig. 20. Barcelona Chair, 1929.
Chromium-plated steel and leather
covered cushions.

Fig. 21. Tugendhat chair.

Fig. 22. Tugendhat couch.

Fig. 23. Glass-top Barcelona table.

Photos courtesy Knoll Associates, Inc.

22

23

Fig. 24. Eero Saarinen. Pedestal side chair.
Molded plastic and metal.
Fig. 25. Eero Saarinen. "Womb" chairs, ottoman,
and table. Chairs of molded plastic and metal,
with foam rubber padding.
Photos courtesy Knoll Associates, Inc.

24

25

26

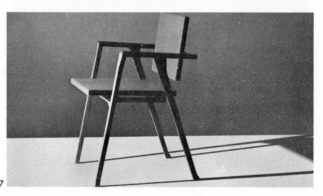

27

Fig. 26. Harry Bertoia. Chairs.

Fig. 27. Franco Albini. "Luisa" chair.
Wood structure with cloth cover.

Fig. 28. Tobia Scarpa. Divan and arm chairs.
Wood frames and leather covering.

28

In the late Twenties, the Russian theater group Vartangov gave a performance in Paris, in which inter-missions were part of the play. Machinists dressed in blue workclothes came onto the stage as the actors left it and, while moving props around, gave a silent mimicry of the previous act. When the others came back, whatever Chinese legend it was about had moved a step higher. The intermission pantomime seemed to be still on, under the profuse words.

So is a still life: an intermission in the human comedy. It is when objects take over and endeavor to speak, in their own way, about the only subject there is: what is this world? what are we? what is reality?

An object is a group of forms and qualities bound by a permanent structure, according to a definite concept. It has a definite personality. With the same concept, different objects are produced—and also remind me of others.

To bring an object to the proscenium, one begins by recognizing its independence from what-ever use we had made of it so far, and by defining it candidly. For every object is functional in several ways, only one of which is utilitarian.

A "flute" of French bread is baked to produce a pleasant food, but also to show it. Its shape is long to provide abundant crust; thin to fit in the hand and to offer easy bites. Cuts have been made on the surface, which fermentation alters a little and which baking remodels: gaping like wounds and like smiles, they reveal the magnificence of the inside, with all the shades of gold between burnt crust and tender dough. It is worthy of the gods, fit for an altar. The finest blind loaf, hygienically packed, is not.

To meditate on this flute is to meditate on the relation of the human hand to divine laws.

But on the easel, bleak, flat, empty, the canvas stands next to the "sumptuous grub," and be-tween them is that void to overcome.

How can the bread be carried across?

What is a painted loaf of bread?

In fact, everything you want, if it sticks to the essential: a feeling of elongation, a staccato of notches and bulges; between those, it is a little strangled . . . Have light fall upon that, and bread is born.

Whether it was carefully brushed up with fine colors or scratched on a wall, or drawn in dust with a finger, is of secondary importance.

"Flute" and "Couronne," 1962.
Photo Marc Vaux.

Table of Loaves, 1952.
Museum, Beauvais.

A jug was one of my best models when, young, unskillful, and poor, I could not convince anyone to sit for me.

I painted it every day, sometimes white, sometimes red: a cylinder running upwards through a ball to a deep mouth on top.

With one finger the potter had pulled the clay to form a beak on one side. On the other side he had pushed and pulled at the same time to form a handle, an arch rather, joining the gaping mouth and the fat belly.

It was night inside. Daylight slid on its flanks. Erect like a column and also slightly human.

I set it on a small table, the traditional thing, with thin legs and one entablature that carried a flat top and hid a drawer. But the real sanctuary was above where I placed the object like a goddess, hopefully.

For I asked that jug to reveal everything, and to answer for man and for the universe.

When I failed to get the message, or rather when I failed to find a language for it, I would get desperate and angry, and fustigate its image with wild brush strokes, shaking the whole picture down, until it cried, until it sang.

A child once wanted to scoop the sea empty and was found to be less of a fool than he who wanted only to understand.

The painter tries to scoop away the mystery that surrounds us using, instead of a shell, one object after another. A choice of objects is like a polygon; a few sides define part of the space and that is already something; the still life does not exhaust the matter but gives, so to speak, a temporary definition of it.

A mature artist is at the same time aware of the futility of his achievement and of the validity of the pursuit.

White Jug, 1928. Collection Georges Bine.

A classification of objects, according to their form and their structure, would constitute a dictionary of visual notions as well as one of ideas.

Somewhere under letter T:

Tuba a): Bunch of tubes. A mess of pipes hitched on to a large blunderbuss.

    This air machine has something of a steam machine: bowels of copper. Through a small cone, a little air enters. Through a large one, it comes out.

    The group of small pipes looks like a Chinese character: a sign; a signal. It wants to be drawn with a brush the size of a finger, and shaped like a drop of melted copper.

    The blunderbuss is architectural, grandiose, a steady volume that can hold the overhanging machinery as well as the considerable sound that is blown through it.

    Push buttons regulate the operations.

Tuba b): If the whole instrument is viewed as a unique volume, another definition follows: it is built out of the contrast between a mass and an intricate set of holes puncturing that mass, between various groups of pipes.

    One would start painting it as a block, then dig, carve out the hollows.

    To finish the picture would be to indicate as a minor characteristic the Chinese sign that was above proposed as the main characteristic.

    To draw a tuba, or to paint it, consoles one for the impossibility of drawing or painting a human figure to complete satisfaction.

    The tuba is a concept, carried into an object, developed in brass, that the painter brings back to the level of human invention, via the fluid medium of color.

    But a head, to be painted, has to be brought down to our level of awkwardness, chopped down to fit our limited means.

    A head cannot be made into an object without abandoning a greatness for which the best works of art express a nostalgia which is in itself perhaps the best we can achieve.

Tuba Lying Down, 1962.

"Tube, Tuba," 1962.

A guitar presents soft forms, going out and in; a handle like a pan and a round hole to see, or to hear, what is dark inside. Melodious flanks, full like hips.

Feminine, descriptively, almost as far as one would care to go. One embraces it in order to play.

A violin is even more feminine, but in this case in demonstration rather than in description. It comes out of the brain of man rather than out of his hands.

The S-shaped holes that are called so suggestively *ouïes* (gills) in French. The round, forceful handle. The sharp ridges, ending in protuberances. A lot there that leads me to think of a skull, that other sound box.

On a stand, side by side, a skull and a violin are kin, somewhere on a conceptual line.

The well-invented violin, an object of great precision made by hand for the ear, sits well next to that dry fruit, molded by a godly thumb. Of the two it is the skull that looks the more manual, made out of a lump of clay, brittle like pottery when it is very dry. Were not the sockets carved out with a thumb? On the surface, many marks, many protuberances could be duplicated only with the fingers.

And the rolled edges the skull shows here and there are far more manual-looking than the polished edges of a violin. In fact, they are very close to those of a freshly opened Rose, that image of God, as the Koran says.

On a round table, a violin, a skull, and a rose. I have placed them with great seriousness following the echo of one into the other, yet with delight and humor.
from academic dullness.

A humor that any serious thought must be able to bear and even to absorb to be alive and free

It is the grin that is macabre, maybe because the teeth already showed in a living mouth and have kept their enamel. They are too realistic. The skull looks better without them.

If one considers them as part of a vertical rhythm, a sort of beat on that long drum, they acquire great significance. The canines articulate the passage from the front of the face to its side. Their line continues in the bone up to the eye socket, and down to the chin.

Vanity with a Rose, 1957.

These plastic considerations deliver us of all lugubrious feelings. One gets beyond the story of a dead person. A small accurately recognized rhythm is part of a wider one, and takes us back to the universe where all cannot but be well, even death.

It may be that we reach here the true sense of the plastic side of Art: to deliver the construction of each object so that it appears as a part of the whole.

From a distance, a skull is a sort of superior crystal, a dwelling place for the brain.

Looking closer at it, one is struck by the intricacy of its arches, the obliquity of its construction. No part is wholly contained in one plane. Everything continues on another side.

Getting farther from it again: the skull is a sort of calabash, with a face stuck on the smaller side and bridged to it by two pairs of arcades.

Here is architecture and also mechanics. It is both divine and human. This is an object at ease among the ordinary objects I daily consult. Yet it is the blueprint of man that became a single man and, later, his funeral monument.

To draw from a skull is to learn to create according to a supreme conduct.

One draws from nature for spiritual discipline as much as for craftsmanship.

On the blankness of this paper, the hand could go in many directions. Only a few of these are endowed with striking visual power. Even fewer mean anything at all.

Placed sideways, the skull wants to roll like a walnut, and the wealth of its structure becomes more impressive than its ominousness.

Two Skulls, 1962. Photo Marc Vaux.

The sawed-off part of a skull forms a handsome cup indeed. The rest, turned upside-down, is like a mountain with a ruined castle on it.

If every object can be considered as a special tool to apprehend "the real," the technique of each painter constitutes a particular tool to define the reality enclosed in each object.

Various painters will not bring the same image out of an object because no technique is capable of embracing the object entirely.

An artist knows his art when he has constructed a technical apparatus that suits his main purpose; however incomplete, he takes his chance with it.

The well-known technique of Japanese lithographers does wonders with certain motifs. Hokusai can give an eloquent image of a carp, a Fuji volcano, a warrior, a cabin in the mountains. He cannot master a skull.

The fluid technique derived from the Chinese lets the object paint itself: flowing water colors will realize flowing elements with the most delicate shadings: waves, mountains, skies.

Looking itself like a hemlock, the tip of the brush gently applied to the paper yields a pine tree.

But the complex reality of the skull is not so easily caught.

The growth visible in the jawbone has something of the flow of a creek, but the construction of the whole and its organic geometry does not fall within the means of the great Japanese artist.

In the skull he takes the mask. He has to count the teeth and create a look in the eye sockets to give them presence. He draws the stitches that join the bones, but omits the powerful bridgework that holds up the face.

On the contrary, when he arrives at the bony hands of a skeleton, so much like branches of a tree, his ability to represent becomes supreme again.

And it may well be this insufficient approach to the structure of a skull that causes most of his faces to be so weak when compared to his magnificent rendering of the clothes and of the general outline of a figure.

Sawed-off Skulls, 1962. Photo Marc Vaux.

The little lead soldier is gray, stiff, and unmonumental. A tiny spool for a torso, a small triangle for the legs, very few details.

Not even the outline is realistic. It was not made from a photograph. It is an idea turned into a primitive fact. A thing that makes me think about a soldier, the way an old stick makes a child think of a gun, harmlessly.

A few brush strokes paint it; a line for the weapon; two or three spots of light, and it lives.

I have often looked with envy at the battle scenes of Gros and Delacroix. Inspiring, breathtaking subjects! Why could not I attempt to paint the Battle of Normandy that has meant our freedom? or the dramatic scenes of defeat we knew in 1940?

It is not so much technically that it is impossible, but morally.

To say that the matter has been exhausted by these great masters would be too easy; war has played less part in their lives than it has in ours.

But, perhaps I could paint, as a still life, a battle of lead soldiers and express there the terrible tragedy of war in an acceptable way.

As if the object, as a filter, had removed some kink, something unbearable about the subject.

Perhaps, in our time, horror can be told only in a very low voice. Keyed down to a diagram.

Lead Soldiers, 1962. Photo Marc Vaux.

Another object looks like an idea of a man.

It stands in a window, arms open, like a maestro. It is meant to teach how one should dress to be successful.

Nothing is less like man; it has to repeat its intention to be one with every detail; molded smile, shining glass eyes, painted eyebrows, toupée; a slight inclination of the head; a twist of the fingers.

Under the magic of artificial lights, it is not an illusion that it creates, but an anti-illusion. It fascinatingly demonstrates what reality is not.

It wears clothes unworn, uncreased, unsold. While a pair of used trousers, with long folds running down from where the waist was to where the shoes could be, tells a lot about humanity, the mannequin says nothing.

It carries a notion of an archetype that appears also in some popular songs. While the singers give voice, gestures, and measure to the dangerously idiotic clichés, it is the onlookers who give some substance to the mannequin by their admiration.

It is not an object one can learn from. No laws play there. It is below everything. It is its complete falseness that brings it to one's attention.

Strangely enough, some eroticism has been instilled into the female mannequin, through a vague nostalgia, or through aloofness: an allusion to what could be artificial in seduction.

With real objects, the mannequin produces a unique contrast. Next to a person, it gives me the feeling of an abyss.

In that absence of reality lies its reality.

Like painters, philosophers search for light. On a higher level, perhaps. From the meaning already gathered in a word, they proceed toward another. From a line to a paragraph and to a page. From one definition to another. From a limited certitude to a wider one. They progress toward solidity and clarity. I admire their rigor; I envy their continuity, but I can follow them only a short way.

Soon I have to return to the motif; to the good object I can love and paw; and that, in turn, I shall have to leave, to manipulate scales of tones on my palette.

The painter works on three different planes. A concept formed in his mind; his eyes discover truth in one object; his hands hunt through the colors a magic path that could bind the concept and the object.

His greatest difficulty is to maintain unity in such different motions.

His greatest advantage is his capacity for holding contradictions together: to him they are oppositions. He knows how to make them the pillars on which an image is built.

Probably, this is not completely clear. All workshop lingo!

It will be the privilege of poets, philosophers, and serious critics to formulate what is finally important, what can be understood, what can last.

But the highest knowledge about Art does not suffice to produce it.

The confused words of the artist, his fumbling, his breaking of categories, his wild trampling over conventions and rules, form the plasma in which the traditions of painting remain alive.

Mannequins, 1950.

A still life begins as a nostalgia of something already seen and forgotten. It grows in the gaps of conscience, where human images are not formed.

As a dog animates part of a house where no one would go, and draws out of us feelings that no person provokes, the object has a capacity for discovery and animation that is its own.

The selection of objects is sensual, unconscious, adventurous. One of them suddenly appears the most important in the world.

Sometimes it is an object that one thought had been exhausted which seems completely new.

I started a new suite of pumpkins because I had discovered a range of tones on my palette where the barbaric red of that fruit found its environment, its harmony.

As soon as it is taken away from the field and brought into the studio, a pumpkin becomes an object.

On a stool, it sits superbly: a glorious sunset.

Ridges show where to cut it. A whole slice will look like some sort of a harp, with weedy strings. Let them be torn away, there remains a moon crescent. Cut in two, it is the cave of Ali Baba. Treasures hang from its cavernous flanks; seedy pearls; juicy agates.

Like any object, the pumpkin is twofold. Something for the belly; something for the imagination. And secrets too, to be hunted. God reveals and hides at the same time.

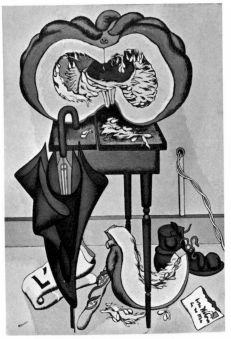

Pumpkin, 1948. Collection Henri Lazard.

Three Small Pumpkins, 1957. Collection Jean Gisbert.

From this "ready-made object"—to speak a little like Marcel Duchamp—to man-made ones: when the object is transparent, when it is conceived so that one sees it functioning, it shows more than itself; it reveals laws that the engineer did not create, but discovered, and used, and with a perfect object, honored.

At the corner of a field, in Belle-Ile-en-Mer, I once met a plow.

In the flat landscape around, under magnificent skies, it sat on its earthly throne, stronger, clearer than anything else.

The big blade dug an unfinished furrow and sailed above it. The polished metal reflected the sky. Far away, on a narrow stretch of sea, other sails seemed to be there only as an echo.

That sort of horsy bicycle holding the machine together; rusted springs coiling under; cables, handles, pieces of harness.

What an object! What a complete still life! What a monument to set on a pedestal in the middle of a city.

They won't do it . . . One paints it, instead.

But it has become a modern fashion to hide what is essential. One shrouds the function of a machine with a sheet of sleek metal, streamlined for no wind.

All hoods down, so to speak.

But when an accident has broken down all protection, when its bowels show up, even in pieces . . . An apocalyptic rhythm runs through and across the hitherto small rhythms of mechanized efficiency.

And I am less impressed by the drama than by the demonstration of power, the same power that made a piston go up and down, but that could not be confined there any longer.

The Rusted Plow, 1957.

"Objets Catastrophés," 1944.
Collection Henri Lazard.

The idea of Apocalypse leads me to the rocks of Belle-Ile that I have painted so often.

Other "ready-made" objects.

Fully abstract structures, built with undecipherable precision by the weather, for the centuries.

Torn away from the earth: one, two, three, four . . . stand the needles of Port Coton.

Apocalypse or Genesis?

Like the skull, but on an enormous scale, each block is produced by clear impulsions, wide cuts, deep carvings, irresistible torsions.

It is at once complex and simple. What a monument also! Down at the bottom, waves make it a fountain.

It is with perfect correctness, with a rigorous sense of continuity that stones like these were set inland, lined from where the sun rises to where it sets, by unknown, religious men.

Rocks of Port Coton, Belle-Ile-en-Mer, 1959. Collection Joseph Cantor.

169

Between the horizon and us, trees, mountains, cities . . . stand as landmarks. Between the void and the easel, objects are lampposts. Placed in a comprehensive order, showing the type and development of their structure, all objects, from the natural needle of stone to the civilized tuba, from a clean hazelnut to the most intricate apparatus in a modern laboratory, would constitute a single, uninterrupted flow. But we meet them as though an infinity of hands had been throwing dice with them.

The artist is born with a definite feeling that Unity exists throughout the incongruous, and that we do not see it only because the links are hidden, or missing, or misunderstood.

He builds still lifes like monuments and like signposts, at the most obscure points of the maze we live in.

Chamber Music, 1960. Collection Maynial.

An object made by men for a definite utilitarian purpose can involve their emotions and thoughts until the object transcends its practical use and takes on qualities of meaning not originally associated with its intended function. The motorcycle has become involved in this way in the lives of some young men of my acquaintance. The following is a report on them and their object. I have written this not as an objective social scientist, but as an involved participant in the phenomenon I wish to describe. I feel I must point out that this paper is not meant to be objective or scientific, but is a report on what some of my friends and acquaintances have to say about their involvement with the man-made object the motorcycle—filled out with a few sympathetic observations of my own.

Out of various needs and their desire to meet and express them men have created a whole universe of objects: objects that serve simply to assist them in the job of survival; objects with no pragmatic role at all; and objects out of whose function there has evolved meaning beyond simple functional performance. The motorcycle, for a group of young men of my acquaintance including, to a degree, myself, has come to fit this last category. Technically speaking, a motorcycle is an open two-wheeled vehicle, usually driven by an internal-combustion engine, for transporting one or two people at a time with a minimum amount of luggage. Yet a friend said: "... you can get to be, y'know, like *friends* with the machine ...," clearly indicating that for him, anyway, a motorcycle was more than a means of transport. It is not an uncommon occurrence that a man's possession should come to mean more to him than was originally suggested by the article's function, and these young men are no exception. They have found something in the motorcycle, beyond its ability to carry them from place to place, that appeals to them very strongly, and has made them, in some cases, something more than mere devotees—"bike-freaks" says one.

Why motorcycles? Why should these young men be attracted to this particular machine, to a machine at all? Can something be learned about them and their lives by what they say about their love of motorcycles, and out of this small sample can any generalizations be made about American man and his relationship to objects of his own making? I think so, for if the selection of people I am describing here is small, at least they must, as

Americans, reflect to some degree the American world, perhaps in a way unique to them as a group, but nevertheless in a way that has grown out of their common involvement in this way of life.

In simpler times a man made a club or a stone ax to meet his needs, and it came to stand for strength, security, and power; and he also had paintings on the walls of his cave which represented something not so simple. Both of these "objects" of his creation tell us something of his outer and his inner worlds. In times such as our own, these two qualities are often found in one object; as the tribesman came to follow certain principles of proportion and decoration in the making of his ax, so has modern man found beauty in the form of his tools. The motorcycle, for this group of young men, is such a tool, representing a great deal beyond its mere function—its beauty and its implicit meanings holding an important place in their lives.

All of these men are very intelligent, some are graduates of the local Boston colleges or other colleges, or have been in college and left. They are involved in automobile mechanics, architecture, silver- and gold-smithing, psychology, painting, and so forth, all are readers and all active thinkers. Their ages run from twenty to twenty-six, and they come from a variety of backgrounds. The one common thread that binds them together is their involvement with motorcycles over several years—an involvement that seems to have extended beyond a teen-age desire for kicks. There was a remarkable congruency in what they all had to say about themselves and motorcycles, and I shall here present their ideas largely in their own words.

Unanimously, they had or desired large powerful machines, and what they had to say about power is a good introduction to their degree of involvement with motorcycles (bikes). One who had a friend's larger machine for a while said:

I had this guy's Norton Atlas for two weeks. I rode it ... I must have ridden a thousand miles on it, without going any place really. I went to S. and back just to loosen it up, dust it off ... oh! ... but ... oh man ... the *power* is just fantastic ... Fantastic acceleration, y'know, I just about put myself off the bike ... People have said that before, but it's an unbelievable feeling.

Photo courtesy of *Action Sports.*

I wanted the funkiest, superdooperist, out-of-sightest motor-cycle in the world because I had become ensnared in the mechanical, emotional, god-knows-what-else-all bag, in which I always contended that the bike I had . . . I wanted to make it go faster, even when it was fast enough that it would kill me. So I figured I can save up my money, get something that's really *top,* y'know, and I'll never see another bike I'll envy the owner of for owning it. And ah . . . I did, and it's true, I haven't.

Another was a bit more analytic:

I certainly would not like a slow bike, I've always tended to get very violent machinery. Violence itself has an attraction, let's face it. Speed is certainly a consideration; power, acceleration, the ability to move around, to be nimble . . .

And others named it love:

. . . I never really understood what had been running through me until I stopped it. It's like seeing a girl very intensely, and then you stop it . . . and there you are, and you look back and see how much it really possessed you.

. . . power, the feeling that you can be hurled forward at a really rapid rate with a kick in the pants, and feel strong enough to control it yourself, and know that you're going faster than everybody else . . . it's a big ego-building thing. And at the same time I don't know if it's because it builds your ego so much or because of the *feeling*, the physical feeling; it overwhelms you, you know, it's like a really exaggerated . . . uh . . . *love*, kind of thing, y'know. Power, and . . . oh man . . . and *what?*

Power, violence, speed, acceleration, and love; Freudian implications perhaps, implications that were joked about:

Certainly, having a nice comfortable fifty horsepower engine between your legs has sexual significance—like, you want the power where the power is . . .

I do not doubt that an analysis could be made of this love of motorcycles in these terms. S. I. Hayakawa took up the subject in regard to the 1957 American automobile. He says:

Even more revealing than horsepower or acceleration is design. First of all there is, of course, the rocket ship motif . . . The seven-year-old cuts box tops from cereal packages and gets himself a space helmet to act out his fantasies. The thirty-five-year-old buys a Plymouth Fury . . .
And to continue on the subject of design, there are the protuberances, the knifelike projections, the gashes, the humps —all dazzlingly colored and outlined in strips of chrome. The symbolism of these is enough to make Dr. Freida Fromm-Reichmann blush—and she doesn't blush easily.●

●
S. I. Hayakawa, "Sexual Fantasy and the 1957 Car," in *Our Language and Our World, Selections from Etc.: A Review of General Semantics, 1953–1958* (S. I. Hayakawa, editor), New York, Harper (1959), pp. 238–239.

Few would dispute this, but a motorcycle does not have such an obvious symbolic role for these men, and though I would be rash to deny the presence of sexual overtones in their attraction to motorcycles, I am convinced by what they say and what I feel that there is a great deal more to it than this. Motorcycles are designed without superficial detailing. The thrill of raw speed and power is generated by the directness of the machinery—not by chrome potency symbols attached to it. The source of the attraction to speed and power may be sexual, but I would be loath to dismiss as only sexual joy at the feel of wind in the face, the sensation of powerful machinery in perfect control, and appreciation of the direct, honest beauty of functional design. So I shall merely accept what was said to me, and leave it to others better equipped to look for unconscious motives.

The love for speed, power, and acceleration generates the pleasure at having this violence in control, at being able to direct and master it. This is no small feat, for the machines favored by this group are indeed violent. They have engines with up to fifty horsepower, they weigh less than four hundred pounds, are capable of top speeds in excess of one hundred miles per hour, and can accelerate from zero to sixty miles per hour in about five seconds. The rider is kept busy controlling all this; his right hand operates the throttle and front brake, his left hand the clutch, one foot operates a lever that changes the gears (of which there are four, and sometimes five), and the other foot operates the rear brake. To get an idea of the violence involved, imagine pushing the gas pedal to the floor in the fastest car and having nothing surrounding you or supporting your back. You would have to hang on for life and continue to operate all the controls—precisely the situation on a large motorcycle. Accelerating too violently on some of these machines will cause the front end to rear up from the ground, throwing the rider on his back with all four hundred pounds of motorcycle in his lap. Needless to say it takes skill and some form of courage to drive these machines —in fact, to really pursue motorcycling as these men have, it takes a good deal of devotion. One man drove one of the most violent of all motorcycles (accelerates from zero to one hundred and fifty miles per hour in nineteen seconds!) over five thousand miles around Europe. He has skill as a driver and relishes it. A man who races said:

I just sort of like going fast. Some people like going fast and they have a skill for it, y'know, a feeling for it, and some don't. I do. It's just like skiing; I like to ski fast, race sailboats in storms and all that sort of stuff. I think it's a very simple sort of challenge-to-the-elements type of thing.

The speed and power of a big machine are impressive and challenge the skill and courage of the rider. As he pushes the machine closer and closer to its limits while holding it perfectly in control, he feels an exhilarating sense of cooperation and man-machine unity. This feeling led many of these motorcyclists to refer to the unity of man and horse:

A good bike with a good rider is very similar to a horse in maneuverability—stop, back up, zorch around a lot. Riding horses is very much a combination effort, like man and machine.

And one man who thought that part of his love for large powerful bikes grew out of a need to compensate for his small size, compared himself and motorcycles to his father and horses:

. . . you know, it's a subconscious thing. It's like Napoleon conquering the world, or something like that . . . My father had the same thing; he used to have the biggest, strongest, you know . . . lightest weight and fastest horses he could . . .

Yet a motorcycle is quite different from a horse, and after thinking over the analogy, one man asked, as if the answer were self-evident, "Would you rather ride a horse or a motorcycle? Let's face it . . . y'know." And I had to admit to the motorcycle.

Why should this be so, and why should these machines in particular have such an attraction? Our civilization obviously depends to a great extent on mechanical equipment; perhaps this climate has fostered within many of us a personal identification with machines, as similarly the Sioux Indians identified with the buffalo, on which their existence depended. In terms of sheer numbers and cultural impact the automobile is our most characteristic machine, but these motorcyclists reject American cars as nothing more than impersonal tools to "beat and throw away." Cars are heavily disguised machines which emphasize comfort and encapsulation in their "styling," depending heavily on the symbolism S. I. Hayakawa has pointed out, as well as on an artificial appearance of speed and power achieved with idioms borrowed from rocketry and aircraft. There is little in the outward appearance of the usual American car to suggest that it is a four-wheeled vehicle driven by an internal-combustion engine that transmits power through a system of gears to the rear wheels. In the recent trend toward so-called sports models, for example, there is a strange air of impotence best characterized by the contrast between the car's external appearance of speed and the soft womb-like, "bucket seats" of the carpeted interior. This is all quite different from a true sports car which is streamlined for speeds that the family car will rarely if ever attain, and has bucket seats which are hard shells designed to support the driver against the violence of motion encountered in racing. As a reaction against machinery so badly distorted as the American car, these motorcyclists have turned to machines which are even more direct than a sports car.

In the motorcycle these men have found qualities of beauty and honesty that attract them, and which by comparison put in relief the anomalies inherent in the American car. The straightforwardness of the motorcycle, and its purity as a functioning machine, make the experience of riding it very elemental and direct. Rushing air and total exposure to environment, as well as to danger, absorb the rider in the sensations and reality of what he is doing, in contrast to a car which protectively transports its riders in a capsule. Most sensations of travel and moving through the environment are lost in a car, and any suggestion of the working machinery is muffled, painted, and chromed out of hearing and sight:

One immediately rejects automobiles as being ugly, gross, dangerous . . . I weigh a hundred and fifty pounds and I don't need three thousand pounds of steel to, like, yank around the city.

I mean you're really aware, aware that there are cars all around, you're aware that there are lights, that that guy's going to hook out on you and so forth . . . you're doing it all. It's not a mindless experience at all. You've got your eyes open, you've got grit in your face . . .

There is nothing more *machinery* than a motorcycle . . . it's *all there,* there's nothing covered up; the engine's doing engine things right there. There is an intimate contact between man and machine; there aren't any plush seats, or pedals to push or all this yadiyada. If you want to shift gears you put your foot in the transmission and kick them around, you know.

Photo courtesy of *Cycle Sport Magazine*.

179

When you travel in a car you're insulated from the environment, you don't feel it. You might as well not be going any place. You can't smell it, you can't talk to people, you can't feel changes in temperature—you're insulated. But on a motorcycle you're not, you're right there, you might as well be taking a trip on a donkey.

. . . mechanized travel in a car is really sort of *degrading*. Man, you're surrounded with a plastic reality, it's a total unreality . . . there's curve-around tinted glass between you and the world, and like all the little padded trinkets reassure you that you're not out in the world, or anything. It closes and you have the very solid *thunk* of the door to encapsulate you. *I* get a very perverse satisfaction in driving a bike through the rain for hours and hours on end . . . absolutely soaked, cold, exhausted, chills; there's a satisfaction to it, same way there must have been riding a horse.

The love for the honesty and directness of motorcycles seemed to dictate an aesthetic in which cars were judged as ugly, motorcycles beautiful. All of the men compared the visual features of different motorcycles, and would often launch into enthusiastic descriptions of the appearance of favorite machines. Where a motorcycle's appearance was preferred over another, the preference usually grew out of admiration for that particular machine's mechanical qualities, as if aesthetic appreciation were entirely dependent on mechanical function. When they might discuss the comparative merits of one motorcycle's type of engine over another's, I never heard comparisons of "styling" as something distinct from the mechanics—as is usually the case when cars are discussed. People often talk about the latest automobile models and their styling, and name preferences in terms of that external quality, venturing not much closer to mechanical considerations than discussing how much horsepower a certain model has, and whether or not to buy power-steering. Motorcycles do not undergo yearly styling changes. In fact, one of the amazing things about the different makes is their consistency over many years. No matter how radically a particular machine is changed internally, the consistency of each company's approach lends a sense of tradition and permanence to their machines—perhaps a further quality of directness and honesty that sets them off against the fickle, consumer-oriented, and annually transformed American car.

I do not want to overemphasize the picture of perfect form-function relationships in this group's motorcycle aesthetic, because they did express some concern for appearance that did not relate directly to function. Though these men honestly do love the functional looks of their machines, there is more to it. Their ideal image of the machine also stems from a general feeling of disgust and deep cynicism aimed at some general falseness of which the American automobile is perhaps only symptomatic. In their praise for the motorcycle there was a tone of defiance, which is perhaps familiar to anyone who has been walking along a road and been stunned by the howl of a motorcycle crashing past, changing gears, and dodging on through traffic. Inherent in this defiance is the other aspect of the motorcycle aesthetic, an aspect not so much concerned with mechanical form-function relationships, as with the motorcyclist-machine in opposition to the-rest-of-the-world relationships. This attitude among these motorcyclists has two features: their ideal of functional honesty, compared scornfully to the general American acceptance of the "plastic reality" expressed in cars; and their self-images as motorcyclists, implicitly in rebellion against the way of life symbolized by the plastic reality. Thus out of their disenchantment has come an image of beauty coupled with an image of defiance and nonconformity. The rider and his machine are seen not only as beautiful, but as more real, and more honest than the image of complacent American man couched in his three thousand pounds of upholstered steel. The speed, the fierceness and violence of the machinery, the grace and coordination of the rider and his motorcycle taking a corner at high speeds, the noise, helmets, leather clothing . . . are all part of the image that opposes the plastic reality; the Goths against the Romans:

It's as if I'm going like *that* to the world . . . you know, it's to people, it's like: "O.K., you think I'm a bikey and I'm going to rape your women . . ." and this kind of thing, and you know, I complied; I had boots and jeans . . .

What an easy way to . . . ah . . . define yourself, what an easy way to establish your difference from other people. Y'know, the point is you don't just ride a motorcycle, you pick up so much with it . . . you pick up the clothes, you pick up an attitude . . . a sound . . . I mean your whole life could be defined simply by riding a motorcycle.

I don't know whether I'm an aesthete or not, but watching a person and a machine going through a bend, a bicycle or a motorcycle, either one . . . I mean scooters are completely ruled out because they're so *uuugly,* you know, they're really ugly, and there is no beauty to them. But to watch somebody take something like a Manx or a G50, which is a really pretty-looking object, and going really fast and just sort of gliding around, maybe even hanging off the bike a bit, is just such a fantastic thing to look at, you know, and such a . . . a . . . ah . . . what's the feeling? Kind of feeling of elation, y'know, if you really dig that kind of beautiful thing.

There is a real sense of hostility. One man somewhat facetiously made it a question of self-defense:

When you drive a bike you have to drive on the assumption that everybody else on the road, in a car, is out to kill you. Not by mistake, but intentionally . . . premeditated murder to wipe you off; collusion, all drivers. This is why there's comraderie among bikies; bikies wave to each other. You know, like, here we are, we're fighting the mammoth.

Another, describing his love for the maneuverability and openness of his machine, ended with a revealing example:

You see a rock in the road in a car, right, and you swerve to the left and miss it; and, like, you don't see it go underneath the car, you don't see it get near the wheels. But, like on the motorcycle you can tick the rock so it goes *dang* and wipes out a pedestrian, or something like that, right?

This was said jokingly, yet it reveals the attitude of "fighting the mammoth." They speak, however, very disparagingly of what one man called the "Saturday Evening Post image" of the motorcyclist—the Hell's Angels, the Marlon Brando style "Wild Ones" who travel in gangs and disturb the citizenry. They choose to express their criticism by building their own world of motorcycles and riding, disturbing or upsetting the people only by being as aloof from them in manner, dress, and appearance as possible—implicit superiority. One man pulls up to the curb in a small town after a long trip:

And then I get off, I'm in full leathers [a protective suit of heavy leather], I've a black helmet, I've a black bike, I have beautiful equipment that just fits me, y'know . . . like I've just come in from a nice little six-hundred mile jaunt on the thing, I take my little typewriter case [for luggage] off the back, park the machine, take off my gloves, my helmet, my goggles, open up my jacket, take out the newspapers I've been using for insulation, open my leather trousers, let the sweat out and the air rises from this incredible heat bath I've been in, y'know. Then I stretch, and I feel very masculine, feel very strong and earthy, intimate with what's happening in my own life, rather than, like, absolutely detached from it. It's nice when other people are watching; I wouldn't say it was a production that was done entirely for my own benefit.

. . . the angle of the bike and your position all very clearly represent the forces involved in the thing; which are, centrifugal force, centripetal force, coefficient of friction of the tires, and gravity. And the angle of the bike is just the result of these forces. When you've got it right, it feels, y'know, it just feels really beautiful.

There is in all this a distinct air of fantasy, where the image of the rebel loner—the ominous figure in leather, hidden behind goggles, climbing off his growling machinery—is reminiscent of the apocryphal Western gunslinger. Yet these men have carried this fantasy beyond the passive dreaming of the movie-goer, and in response to some strong drive in their lives, have found in the motorcycle the chance to express the feelings that cause us all to have picaresque daydreams.

I believe that all these men to some degree feel choked by the "plastic reality" of their world. As they move about and play their roles in life they feel themselves as unreal, in some way out of touch with the reality of natural and physical sensation; they feel that our culture somehow suppresses the energy and potency of their individuality. It is this the motorcycle helps them overcome.

Motorcycles are machines, man-made, controlled by men, and expressions of human skill and mastery of tool-making. Like the cave man's ax, the motorcycle is made by men who wanted to form a tool that directly, most efficiently, and with no wasted time, effort, or material did that for which it was intended. The user of such a tool can go into his environment, and meet it masterfully; the tool is an extension of himself, amplifying but not replacing his own strength. An example of this can be found in the way men once waged war. When a samurai drew his sword and strode into battle he was not turning the job of fighting over to his sword: *he* did the fighting, and the sword, the result of many centuries of refinement for its task, was an extension of his own power. Now we look on the samurai sword as a beautiful object, its simplicity and the perfection of its curve somehow expressing the quintessence of a sword's quality. We forget that it was a very real and brutal tool that hacked with extreme efficiency into men's flesh, serving the strength and skill of a trained killer. Now wars are fought by machines; the pilot of the jet bomber does not see himself as a killer, but as an extension of his machine, the possessor of certain skills that are needed to assist the metal monster in its job of killing. As the guided missile replaces the bomber, even that element of contact is lost, and we suddenly find ourselves afraid that the machine itself autonomously will bring destruction upon us—we are not really sure we are its master. This removal from personal responsibility for

Photo courtesy of *Action Sports.*

our modern forms of killing is symptomatic of something general in our world, and has its most frightening form in the huge missile system.

In our present cultural environment the machine has come to protect us from exposure to the feelings and meanings of our day-to-day existence. We place the simplistic world of the television tube between ourselves and reality. We build buildings that are sealed from the outside and create their own weatherless environment—no breeze through a window on a hot day. And we allow ourselves to be transported from place to place in cars that carefully remove all sense of travel, replacing it with artificial sensations, and traffic jams. Our tools, instead of heightening awareness of reality by giving us the means to meet with larger segments of it, and so feel ourselves expand through their functioning, disguise what they are doing, how they do it, and to what they are doing it—and the scope of our existence shrinks. An exception are the tools for the exploration of space. As they move us further and further from our world we must learn to include in our sense of reality the notion of our smallness, and the infinity of space around us. This stirs something in all of us, and we find ourselves involved in every moment of the astronaut's experiences.

These motorcyclists feel that their machines give them a voice by setting them apart from others as "bikies." Motorcycles do not try to be any more than what they are, look like no more than what they can do, and they carry the rider through the wind and over the roads so that the act of riding is so fine an experience that the achievement of movement from one place to another becomes almost secondary. Each one of these motorcyclists gets pleasure from the act of controlling his machine, and each is able to understand what his machine does and can fix it when it needs repair. Each has found that his machine has beauty which is not deceitful, and can be relied upon to be honest and direct in its functioning. The motorcycle and riding it are more than anything else felt to be real.

Then I stretch, and I feel . . . very strong and earthy, intimate with what's happening in my own life, rather than, like, absolutely detached from it . . .

. . . being in contact with your reality is so much a fine thing.

Photo courtesy of *Action Sports*.

People who make things can be divided between those who have qualms about what they do and those who find reflection a hindrance. The latter are probably religious people who feel that they should not question their gifts, and they doubtless have qualms that are stifled, while those of the former case are generally uncomfortable without a theory. But being no more than an image-maker's review of his current situation, this really cannot claim to be a theory.

The word *qualms* could be expanded into penalty-for-curiosity. A man-made object has a way of revealing itself to be something else than it at first appears, and then *that* revelation proves to be a cover story, and the whole process of undraping the truth is a disturbing one, subject to unaccountable blockages. The printmaker John Paul Jones says that he catches himself trying to look around the edge of a canvas or plate, to see what it exists to conceal. And if we create a non-object, isn't this the deepest concealment of all? This is a freedom due precisely to our not being observed creating—for we see nothing that can watch us.

We are talking about paintings, and nothing but paintings, with the justification that the creation of something other than the world given us seems here most complete: we can have not only a new object but new space—the original Heaven and Earth could be removed and the world of art would remain. Paintings have become man-made objects *par excellence* (although they always were man-made) by dint of now being nothing else.

It would seem that we have finally reached an end result in man-madeness; and yet whenever in art we have a sense of end it can be taken as proof that we have come to another beginning. The current end result suddenly appears as a scene of expectation, the setting of a stage, a curtain rising on the set, the preparation of a field in which something is to take place. This is not to cry down the work of two decades because of a feeling for change; on the contrary, what is good enough to *be* painting becomes the most valuable of the raw materials for those who want to paint more.

To progress through a figure of speech: apparently we now believe that a star or planet is formed by the condensation of dust particles; a critical dustiness is reached in a cosmic cloud, and an inward pull takes over. To get to this point is no small feat. Perhaps this is the conception moment of a universe, from which everything follows. An analogous condition seems to have been reached on canvas, and perhaps it could only be reached on canvas, for neither architecture nor sculpture can be sufficiently void. If one thinks of our current painting in the aggregate (an insult to every individual painter, but we live in aggregates), the impression is of rarefied space (yet less rarefied than non-man-made space) of such a condensation that it cannot help going on to be still more condensed. Some object seems due to appear, and heat up in the process, until this concretion takes on a life of its own.

Our figure of speech is now overplayed, as though we were really describing a cosmic trend, whereas we are only talking of what someone is likely to do. But let us save something of our image—an initial weightlessness. A capital letter on a page has no weight in the literal sense that a picture *of* something gets involved with our earth-bound experience of gravity. The capital letter is simply there because it was put there for another person to find. It is afloat, it will not drop. And if gravity is involved, it is simply the object's own attraction. The object behaves like a heavenly body, one of the core images in Kandinsky's compositions.

Our capital letter escapes terrestrial gravity because it exists in another world, that of symbolism. It refers to something else which it does not altogether hide. It is a name for something else that is nameless. And on and on, palimpsest upon palimpsest. But after we have watched symbols at their progressive concealing and revealing, we can stop the game by saying that the object only conceals itself. It is in temporary disguise.

Leave it so for the moment. We can now discard one expectation about it, or one project if we are thinking as a *maker*. The last thing to be expected is an architectural painting—a post-Cezanne painting. And for the good reason that terrestrial architecture still means gravity, in spite of all *pilotis,* and gravity means a working frame on which the image must sit, when what is required is not geometry, but a field of force self-centered, surrounded by discontinuity.

The preparation of such a field, such a near-void, seemed to require the large canvas. If the angle of vision were sufficiently wide, the border transition to the non-art world needed another act of attention, a refocusing which abolished the original seeing. And so the painting established its own nonlocation. The large painting is the very opposite of mural painting: it is large not to adapt itself to architecture but to obliterate architecture. The architecture of a moving-picture house cannot make a film better or worse. It has in fact to destroy itself, by retreating into nonarchitectural darkness, so that the film becomes the universe. Yet one may doubt that the large canvas is with us for long, for monstrosity always has a reason, but it is usually an awkward one, and evolution shrugs off bigness as quickly as possible; nothing vanishes more swiftly, or in retrospect seems more bizarre, than the gigantic.

The absence of frame is part of this establishing of an indefinite border. The immediate wall becomes the sea of ice with which early cartographers capped the known world. With white walls, and frameless paintings, good installation is simply good pagination, and the painting turns into a color plate—often more valuable to the editor-installer than the painting itself. Now a page has space of a sort, just as a book contains time of a sort, but primarily it is a territory of ideas, and making a page large as a wall does not make architecture. In installation this was a good solution, precisely because the painting now *was* on a huge page, and not on a wall.

Nor is the partition serving as page the only way in which this discontinuity can be established. There is an actual circumstance where architecture provides this amorphousness, this fluidity, although it is digression, just as this paragraph is a digression. The Guggenheim Museum gives the impression that Wright was willing to commit suicide if only he could destroy painting, and yet he has created a fluid *nowhere* that provides the essential release which our paintings have been demanding. Even the floor melts from under foot, all is disturbingly unstable and hallucinatory, and suddenly the only architectural leftover is in the square corners of the canvases. Canvases here should shape up like television screens, for if we are projecting out of our minds, do we not sense our minds as living in a round place, a cave whose opening is vaguely visible to us as an eye socket, or the just-seen rim of spectacles?

Now to return to our field without definite limit, and our awaited image within it. Only suppose the image to have a life of its own, to exist, and we are at once freed of constructing it. It is *emergence* that we expect. To compose becomes an arrogant word if we are simply coming into focus.

A lantern slide comes on the screen, all color and glow. The projector is quickly focused, and what was Matta becomes Monet. Whether or not this is gain, the clearing up of an image is at once relief and revelation. If we have reason to believe that the image is *there,* we are obliged to help it into being. What bothers is that Monet had to appear, when we wanted something not seen before. The great excitement of contemporary painting is the sense of becoming, and how can we escape the hankering for novelty, if we feel that the things we contemplate (or make) are in disguise?

Consider a painting by Philip Guston of a year or so ago: a gray field with some central heavier congestion in linear red. To me, this handsome abstract painting became, one day, the convincing image of the retina itself, for I had once had to diagram retinas with enlarged blood vessels for an uncle who was a physician. This, of course, sheds no light whatever on Guston's reputation, unless we imagine that objects in disguise are more compelling than objects in the clear, and we should expect any such intrusive private explanation to be resisted by the artist, for if he had consciously meant to paint a retina he would doubtless have gone further and seen something on it or in it. But here is a step in the direction I want to be going; it gives me an image (the retina) of the capacity to see an image.

If we are waiting in some pictorial pre-dawn for an image, we must mention Rothko's painting. This does not mean that his canvases tempt the vandal to creep up and provide the image. I recall Rothko breaking out an early painting of stick figures in a subway; he set this canvas sideways so that a figure became a thin horizontal division, to make clear the resemblance to his later paintings. To me, this suggested that the figures were still there in the divisions between tonal areas, no less *there* because they were suppressed.

It is natural to select examples which brace a point of view and to force support out of them, so we had better turn to a less reticent painter—what about Pollock, surely an artist central to our time. Although we have made use of the galactic figure of speech, and this figure has almost been set aside for Pollock, his paintings to me are much more of a stirred broth, a weed-strewn Sargasso Sea, a sea-deep breeding ground. The only time I saw Pollock was on a rainy summer afternoon, tension charged with idleness—it was not too long before he died. I was brought into a Henry Millerish scene: the three people with him rounded out a foursome that suggested Mexico City: one encountered the vitality of scrawled black hair, glistening against the dim wet green from outdoors. We were taken out to the barn studio, and Pollock obligingly unrolled a long canvas on the floor: here was the same pubic hair scrawl. At the same time, since we had been picking our way across a watery lawn, the painting had a wonderful wet coiling stagnation about it, as though it could still be stirred if Pollock were not stagnant too. In the house, a new canvas on the wall was of large, fierce, ghoulish heads, as though some carnival were in preparation. So this was what was to come. Only it didn't.

To come to the point, I cannot avoid the belief that the image that will emerge will ultimately make itself clear as a self-image. We are looking in a clouded mirror. It is ourselves we shall see.

Let us not imagine settling down to a life of self-portraiture. We are, I take it, a residuum of experience, which we explore in reverse. This is the artist's contribution: he faces upstream *toward* life, and so fights time and death, while all the others are going their chronological way, which they curiously think of as forward. The fishing is best in those eddies of near-memory where nothing is quite clear. It is a very difficult thing to find the right place between the yet-to-be-remembered and the rational. Take Kandinsky—how much better in the 1910's than the 1920's—because how much nearer Kandinsky. He had created a cosmos that was a fertilized egg held up to the light, a pulsing heart in its center, with blood vessels and nerves shooting out and in. That was better than being fertilized by architecture. Did the Bauhaus persuade him that he was Pythagoras, and flatter him with circles and triangles into the belief that he was going ahead?

Private myth made visible is not fairy tale. The perpetual childhood in Chagall is discouraging —we can only be a rooster for so long. We do not need to remain children because early memory explains us as adults and so nourishes us. The final metamorphosis out of childhood provides the purity of faith in Chagall's Old Testament prints: this is the childlike fulfilled.

Myth is a very old tired word, but no matter, for that very reason it has a stronger hold on the past. It turns our attention back. We should ask ourselves whether there is a history behind our expectations whenever we are bemused by a sense of discovery. Of course there is history behind the images here postulated, a history illuminated by embarrassingly great names—but that is always the case when the past is evoked, for only the great are alive. For an eternity of self-images free from gravity there is the Sistine Ceiling, over-compartmented, to be sure, a constriction finally banished in the *Last Judgment*. Then we go to Venice. Nothing is more to our purpose (historically, not for now) than Tintoretto —for example, his *Bacchus and Ariadne*. This is a complete image emerging from a void that is water-air-amniotic fluid: an indeterminate field of flotation. It was a time of literary myth which required an appearance remote from our needs, but what is important is the extent to which the Venetians were water-borne, afloat. Even their architecture floats on the sea, and is consequently quite unreal, and simply brushed in. Venetian architecture did not threaten or confine the canvas, and so Venetian painting had no limit. The discontinuity was provided by the invention (or capture) of water vapor in paint.

If we follow this atmosphere, the atmosphere that oil made possible, to Spain, we find the now much publicized "image of man" standing upright in a solitary void, in a gray-brown Purgatory that contains a life. Velazquez is pure mirror painting: here is a box of dim air, finite, yet incommensurate. It is hard to image such a ground or field existing without a figure stepping into it, as though the conditions of life had just been created. The importance lies in just this ground or field, without which Velazquez could not exist. With this, the important thing right now is the ground or field that has been prepared for us, all established for the emergence of an image.

We cannot go on from here wherever atmospheric painting leads us. For soon too many objects appear; and then a scene clears up. The Dutch, except for Rembrandt, were too interested in possessions, and kept shop. Even in Rembrandt clothes are possessions—we are touched by the early vanity and late poverty—while for the Spaniard they were part of a spiritual definition.

Head and two hands give us three images for one, and that is what clothes do: by concealing all else, they create a tension (sexual because of concealment) between a head and two hand satellites. It is amazing that this little solar system remained stable for so long, that a head was simply content to see itself as a head, considering the record it kept within it, that a hand simply re-created itself as an idle hand. The portrait of Gertrude Stein was perhaps the last portrait in this sense. Picasso took eighty sittings (was it?), doubtless in an effort to get his own head into the canvas instead. But she managed to freeze him out, and after that he gave us only himself. After that, all is Picasso, which is obviously how he wanted it.

It is disturbing to contemplate Picasso for anyone looking to the emergence of an image in his own labors, for Picasso so patently wore the image out, progressively worrying it to death. And he seems so untroubled, he does not disturb himself like the Expressionists. The Spaniard's natural acceptance of death makes courage an absolute and not a relative thing, and he does not scare himself. A view of man as life and death, and not just life, makes for a special focus, and all adjacent things become properties better discarded in the big scenes. Instead of conscious and unconscious (our twentieth-century dichotomy) there is visible and invisible.

But we *are* in the twentieth century, and what Picasso offers us is conscious-unconscious to us, whatever it may be to him. These two have to be fused, and this is the composition. The one natural fusion of these two, at least the healthy natural resolution of their tension, is in laughter. So if we are not to end in tragedy we must end in comedy, and Picasso has had the health to end with farce.

We should remember that Picasso's images are quite concrete, essentially sculptor's images set before us in the round, and if this adds a certain Surrealist conviction, basically it comes down on the side of sanity and limits alarm. Since Picasso's images are as much there as the figures in store windows, they have just that restriction on their capacity to haunt. They lack the witchcraft quality of Goya, whose images are so much more strange, even when so much more recognizable, an effect due in part to our uncertainty about their scale (once we know that a giant is possible for Goya), an effect which could not be managed without atmosphere. The *Third of May* would not be so frightening if it were not for the quality of the dark sky. In the etchings, the terror is the work of Goya, but aquatint made it possible. Having argued so far in favor of dusk, Goya, and the indeterminate, over the Picasso sculptural, Picasso must be allowed his exception (which he can always manage) in *Night Fishing at Antibes*. This is a tremendous painting, far more shocking than *Guernica,* and the uncertainty out of dusk is a potent element in the means assembled. We are talking about a special quality of field or ground, of low illumination in which something can appear. Here Picasso and Goya are close.

To jump all the way from the black paintings of Goya to the black paintings of Ad Reinhardt: here are canvases that are paintings in the Goya sense in that they require an attention which cannot be extended to the room. They are not really in the room, and so have nothing to do with decoration. The tensions and gradations here submerged become significant exactly to the extent that they are almost below the level of perception. It is the sense of something found, detected, which disturbs, and offers the possibility—and hence the necessity—of another sort of life. This is something that could hardly have happened early in the development of abstract painting; and just because it suggests the lateness of the style it becomes a portent. The merest hint of something there, in a field adequately sensitized for its discovery, sets up a Helen Keller equivalent to normal seeing.

Again, I am sure this is seeing something in Reinhardt's work which is not intended, and that the artist can hardly be willing to have used as a point of departure. Yet that is what happens to every artist in a time when art grows out of art. To look at a Reinhardt painting brings me nearer to seeing what I want to see.

So much should suggest that our image will not have the look of an image "returning" or an image that the waiting model-mongers are to take over. If we expect a head, we may get the whole conglomerate of experience, or vice versa. An artist painting for other artists may be through when he makes clear what he has in mind. The overdefined goes on to be absurd. Because a thing, any thing, has no meaning unless it refers to some thing, or (at last) to some unannounced aspect of itself. We cannot go further, and so we can always go further. For an ultimate symbol is a contradiction in terms, which should keep us at work in some humility. This essay then is perhaps simply an expression of gratitude that we are where we are; for the emergence of a symbol is a kind of ceremony that requires preparation.

If the image is slight, or if its power of emanation is weak, that is all right, in fact, that is good, so long as it is an active image, an active source. For the image is *us,* and should be alive, and we should be where it is. This is the very opposite of the *scene* in paint, which was a passive experience for someone standing outside. The great trouble with the scene in paint was precisely its passivity.

We saw everywhere and everything, because everything was coming on in. The image we are talking about must take us into itself, and being ourselves need not project far, for we are not all-powerful. It need not ever reach its frontier, the frame. It is enough for it to loom into being, and so establish itself.

For instance, the writer is at present concerned with moons and suns because they conveniently hang in the canvas, and are simply there, with some radiation of their own. Given a chance, they distort themselves into stand-ins for heads, those heads which we began by trying to draw. They are globular selves. And this is not as solipsistic as it sounds. An image that has its history within it is not meaningless. Open the eighteenth-century volume of Cook's *Voyages,* and cross the Pacific raising a totally new island every day, and naming it for someone aboard until every man had his island. Each island was never the same again, for it had entered history, and it took its namesake into history in return. It is a curious thing, the voyager being assigned such a random image of himself, for the island was to be his future. Every man *is* an island; but we are part of an archipelago.

No object, man-made or natural, can resist the on-slaught of the imagination. If you determine to "think" an object—cup, bottle-drier or jet engine—how long can you keep the image intact? Not very long. Within a matter of instants the restless imagination has begun its errant voyage into a sea of associations, drawing the rational mind like a dory behind it, away from terra firma. Once the imagination is invoked, the common-sense idea of the object as something that resists is only valid for a moment.

Given the expansive tendency of the imagination, the question of man's relationship to objects is easily answered: it does not change. Objects are always signals to the imagination to begin its work. They are furnishings of the mind's eye.

There is a subtle difference, however, between the reveries inspired by the hand-fashioned object and those dependent on the object produced en masse by machines. When Homer wrote his elaborate description of Achilles' shield, he referred not only to the physical characteristics of the object but implicitly to the imagination of the object's creator, Hephaestus. As he hammered and modeled and forged, Hephaestus spun out his own reveries. In Homer's minute description of the five sections of the shield, each detail is catalogued objectively—the ploughed fields, the dancing maidens, the herds and shepherds, the vineyards and walled cities. But he went further. He paid tribute to the narrative of Hephaestus who first sketched the cosmos ("the earth, the heavens and the sea and the unwearying sun and the moon waxing to the full") and then fashioned the shield with much cunning from his "wise heart." For Homer, the object is at once a work of art with specific physical characteristics, a work of historical documentation, a work of another man's imagination, and a signal for his own. Here, then, we have the man-made, handmade object in various relationships—an interaction between artists secure in the knowledge that whatever there is to be contemplated has sprung from a kindred imagination.

The object the contemporary artist contemplates is usually anonymous and one of many of its kind. No other creative imagination must be taken into account. There is no fraternal message from one imaginative elite to another. A sports car or a lawn mower can be admired and described, but there is no communion be-tween its originator and the artist dealing with it. The artist's relationship to the machine product is direct, blunt.

The Industrial Revolution was viewed with anxiety by the nineteenth-century artist who voiced his fear of the proliferation of machine-made objects. He despaired in the presence of so much anonymity and felt the machine encroaching on him, spewing forth its countless products and, in its clamor, drowning out the individual voice. Flaubert hated the machine age and felt it would coarsen the people and make them incapable of understanding the arts. "What can you expect of a population like that of Manchester which passes its life making pins? And the confection of a single pin needs five or six different specialities! Work subdivides itself putting beside the machines a quantity of machine-men."[1]

In the visual arts the machine menaced originality, or so the nineteenth-century theorists contended in England where they busied themselves with the Arts and Crafts Movement. They set up workingmen's colleges designed to teach the factory worker the elements of taste and design (a Utopian scheme repeated in the twentieth century at the Bauhaus with equally ambiguous results). Even Ruskin worried about the workingman's loss of taste and arranged to have his *Stones of Venice* printed in a cheap edition for laborers, in the hope that they would understand the superiority of the old hand methods of construction.

Disturbed by the Industrial Revolution, artists responded by excoriating the bourgeoisie. Tracts against utilitarianism abounded in the second half of the nineteenth century. Realists and symbolists alike deplored the effect of industry on society. In the welter of discussion, two dominant attitudes emerged. One was that the artist could flee from the blight of industry and its products, taking refuge in a fantasy world in which the objects were pure and worthy of contemplation. This is the course Flaubert took when he wrote meticulous descriptions of antique jewels in *The Temptation of St. Anthony* and *Salammbô*. The other form of defiance was to use the new machines and machine-made objects in works of art, subordinating them to the private vision of the artist. This is what the Impressionists and later the Cubists did.

Artists opting to face reality—or so they thought—and accept the miracles of technology as miracles, entered the twentieth century with an exhilarated vision of a new life for art. The idea of a "new spirit" gained hold, making it possible for the artist to develop fresh attitudes toward utilitarian objects previously despised. The "realistic" attitudes of the early Cubists was expounded by Guillaume Apollinaire. He explained repeatedly that the Cubists wanted to paint the "objective reality" of their objects. Everyone has to admit, he wrote, that a chair from whatever vantage point one sees it never ceases to have four legs, a seat, and back. If one deprives it of one of these elements, one deprives it of its essentials. The Cubists, in restoring the four legs, he said, created a human and poetic painting.[2]

One of the most important advances, according to Apollinaire, was the Cubists' reference to the environment of the modern city, incorporating its posters and advertisements in their work. Defending their use of common materials, he wrote that "one can paint with what one likes . . . it is enough to see the work; it is by the amount of work which goes into it that one measures the value of a work of art."

The Futurists, also intent on the industrial realities, had proclaimed similarly that the artist should avail himself of new materials. Boccioni in his 1912 Manifesto of Futurist Sculpture urged sculptors to use modern materials such as cement, steel, iron, mirrors, and electricity. But Apollinaire attacked the Futurists for their romanticism and said that their wish to paint a state of the soul could only lead to illustration. The Cubists, Apollinaire felt, were establishing a new art in which illustration gave way to "pure painting." (In this Apollinaire confusedly sensed a later development when Mondrian would declare still another new reality: the pure painting as an object in itself.)

The new aspect of objects in painting was signaled by Apollinaire in a 1913 newspaper analysis of Picasso's work. Sometimes, he wrote, Picasso used authentic objects such as twopenny songs, real postage stamps, and fragments of newspaper, adding no picturesque element to the truth of these objects. The objects used had "already been impregnated with humanity for a long time." For Apollinaire and the men of his epoch, the use of common objects was based on their affective value. That is, each selected material was valued for its association, for the degree with which it was impregnated with human use.

Many avant-garde poets maintained a positive attitude toward the commonplace object in the early twentieth century. Jean Cocteau thought that the job of the poet was "to strip bare, under a light that shatters our indifference, the surprising things around us which our senses register automatically. . . Put a commonplace in place, clean it, rub it, light it so that it will give forth with its youth and freshness the same purity it had at the beginning and you will be doing the work of the poet."[3]

For Cocteau, it was still necessary to clean and light his object, thereby performing the time-honored task of metaphorical adjustment. For many artists reacting against the acceleration of technology, putting the commonplace in place took a different form. They continued the stubborn romantic tradition of absolute resistance. Marcel Duchamp registered the most intransigent protest when he invented the notion of the ready-made. In his opposition to *embourgeoisement*, Duchamp adopted an ironic mode of expression which, despite the dense mystification surrounding his work that he encouraged, clearly stems from the ironic romanticism of the nineteenth century.

The ready-mades were "selected" in New York between 1914 and 1925. They are an overt indictment of the anonymity enforced by assembly lines. When his urinal signed "R. Mutt" was rejected by the Salon of Independents in New York in 1917, Duchamp wrote: "Whether or not Mr. Mutt fabricated the fountain with his own hands is not important. He has *chosen* it. He has taken an ordinary element of existence and disposed it in such a way that the utilitarian significance disappears under the new title and the new point of view—he has created a new thought for this object."[4]

As Marcel Jean has remarked, Duchamp's ready-made is a development of the principle of banality. "In these disconcerting objects, the personality is founded on the most vast generality, the collective fact becomes the unique example."[5]

Duchamp's ironic dismissal of the manufactured object, and his hint that the artist would no longer be able to cope with such realities—the implicit argument in the ready-mades and in his own withdrawal from art —was paralleled by the Dadas in Europe. They took flight from the plethora of industrial objects by investing them with ironies. Dada objects were intended to be nonsensical parodies of nonsensical reality. Acute consciousness of the machine perfection of death-dealing tools in World War I led the Dadas to bitter denunciations of *petit bourgeois* materialism. When they incorporated shreds of daily life in their work they did so with a dual and often equivocal purpose—both to deride and explore.

Yet their attitude was not so different from that of the Cubists. They still believed (as did Duchamp for that matter when he proudly declared that he, Duchamp, had *chosen* the urinal after all) the artist expressed his individuality in his choices. Kurt Schwitters wrote that "every artist must be allowed to mold a picture out of nothing but blotting paper, provided he is capable of molding a picture."[6] With Apollinaire, Schwitters took the stand that only the artist can make free with new materials, only he who can mold a picture in the first place can put the commonplace in place.

1. Marcel Duchamp, *Fountain.*
Galleria Schwarz, Milan. Photo Bacci Attilio.

2. Raoul Hausmann, *Mechanical Head,* 1918.
Collection Mrs. Hannah Höch, Berlin.

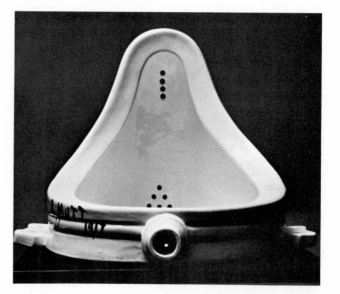

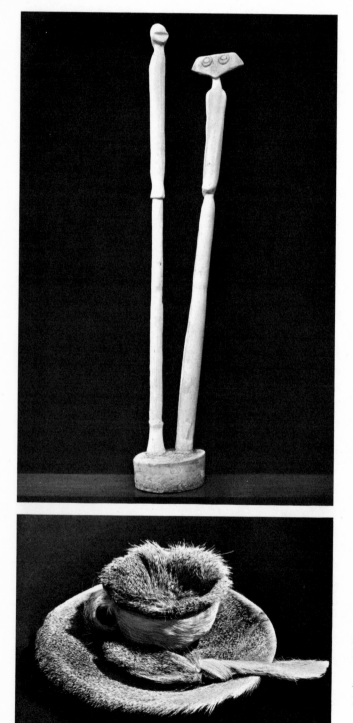

The Dadas' successors, the Surrealists, eluded the commonplace with an aristocratic *élan* equal to Flaubert's. When they dealt with objects they sought to create, through the classical technique of juxtaposition, a hybrid having both objective and subjective qualities. Few of the items exhibited in the *Exposition surréaliste d'objets* in 1936 were intended to display the reality of the commonplace. Even those untouched "finds" such as fossils, shells, biscuits, and roots in context with neighboring exhibits tended to vivify the imagination and serve as talismanic evocations of decidedly non-commonplace experience.

At bottom the traditional poetic technique of metaphor, of juxtaposed entities underlay Surrealist theory. From the famous Lautréamont encounter, *"Beau comme la rencontre fortuite sur une table de dissection d'une machine à coudre et d'un parapluie,"* they were able to move far afield in a poetic fantasy of objects, transforming them often into literary metaphors. They were as classical as Mallarmé, whose "objects" were penetrated by an extraordinary subjective intelligence; as Proust, whose involuntary memory invested objects with a wealth of associations; as Joyce, whose objects, like those of Picasso, were "impregnated with humanity."

Up to this point in twentieth-century art, the object is still subordinate to the artist who focuses on it. All of these "isms" refract reality through personal visions. All of them purport to re-present an environment, either through a fresh look at its commonplace furnishings, or through a psychological insight into the other reality, that of dreams. Whether rejecting objects or incorporating them, the artists still took pride in their cleverness, their individuality, their ability to sift and select from the welter of things in their experience.

3. Max Ernst, *Lunar Asparagus,* 1935.
Museum of Modern Art, New York.

4. Meret Oppenheim, *Fur-covered Cup,* 1936.
Museum of Modern Art, New York.

5. Man Ray, *Mr. Knife and Miss Fork,* 1944.
Galerie Rive Droite, Paris.

6. Alan Kaprow, *Panels,* 1957–1959.
Solomon R. Guggenheim Museum, New York.

As the century wears on, the circumstances which fostered negative attitudes—technological advances and concomitant menaces to human values—become more insistently disrupting. Artists who weathered World War II had none of the blithe confidence in the effect of their personalities that, despite everything, still belonged to the pre-World War II artist. The artist today often suspects that he is engaged in a losing battle with the effects of mass production, and above all, with the bourgeoisie and its materialism.

His response is often extreme. A resurgence of Ubuism marked the 1950's with a throng of disaffected individuals seeking to escape from all tradition, including the traditions of protest. *"Nous n'aurons point tout démoli si nous ne démolissons mêmes les ruines!"*[7] Would Père Ubu have turned a hair if he had seen with what dedication the mid-twentieth-century artist set about destroying even the ruins?

The Dadas had left a few things undone, among them, the total destruction of the notion of Art. Ever since the late nineteenth century there has been an irascible nucleus of artists who associated art with decadence and materialism. That a work of art is purchased, fondled, and viewed as a symbol of status is taken to mean that there is something fundamentally wrong with a work of art. Faulty as this logic may be, a great many serious young artists operate within it.

In order to answer history and to maintain a distance from involvement with the bourgeoisie, certain artists have taken to using perishable and fragile objects in their creations. The use of food which rots, or papers which wither, or plastic bags that burst is common in the hybrid theatrical "happenings" in New York. The pathos inherent in all such aesthetic demolition acts rings out in the words of one young artist who sees himself embattled in "a trying period," and who righteously underlines that there can be no "rewards" for these hybrid, ephemeral works.[8] No collector will debase them.

Extremist aesthetic attitudes exact what I would call an impoverishing diminution of choices. If choice and decision are the bases of a work of art, as I believe they are, the new tendency reduces the number and quality of decisions to a minimum. More and more the artist relinquishes the proud role of master of his material; more and more he gives way to those very techniques which he opposes.

The diminution of choices is given a positive value by artists who have come to regard Chance as an answer to the symmetry and maddening regularity of machine culture. In the hands of Max Ernst gratuitous inspiration thrives. Yet in his ironic voice, there is a touch of pride in his superiority which identifies him as a child of the early part of the century: "Surrealism permitted painting to remove itself with seven-league-boot strides from the three apples of Renoir, the four asparagus of Manet, the little chocolate women of Derain and the package of cigarettes of the Cubists . . . that, of course, to the great despair of art critics who are alarmed to see the 'author' reduced to a minimum, and the conception of 'talent' annihilated."[9]

Ernst's wry attitude is significantly altered when adopted by many younger artists. The "objective" world, the real world of meaningless accumulations of things, has overtaken them and the irony germane to the Surrealists is out of place. I doubt very much that Max Ernst would seriously think of himself as an untalented do-it-yourself chap who came upon his discoveries quite by accident. His accidents are always transformed. But in the newer aesthetics of the past few years, Accident and Chance are invested with a supreme value and the "author" is straight-facedly allotted a rather minor role.

The nightmare of poet Henri Michaux, who imagines himself surrounded by hostile objects pressing in on him and seeking to displace his "I," to annihilate his individuality by "finding their center" in his imagination, has become a reality for many artists. The profusion of things is an overwhelming fact that they have ruefully learned to live with.

The art world is a small reproduction of the great world, repeating its gestures and foibles. Perhaps it would be in order to point out here that since World War II, the choices available to the individual in all areas appear to be diminishing at a rapid pace. The surge of interest in machine-made objects and in the chance assemblage of them, and the pursuant reduction of choices, is probably easier seen in a sociological light than an aesthetic one. The whole emphasis on junk culture and popular art is saturated with extra-aesthetic considerations.

The idea of a junk culture vigorously argued by the British critic Lawrence Alloway is based, as he says, "on

7. Max Ernst, *Painted Collage,* 1963. Alexander Iolas Gallery, New York.

8. Max Ernst, *Aeolian Harp,* 1963. Alexander Iolas Gallery, New York.

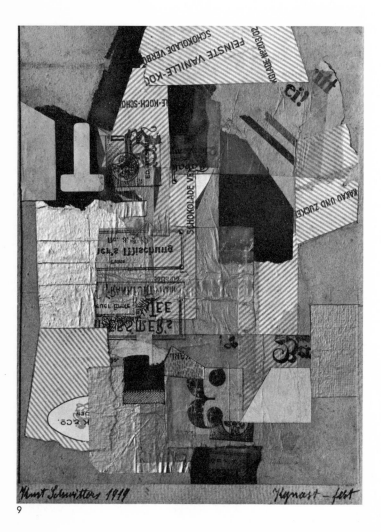

9

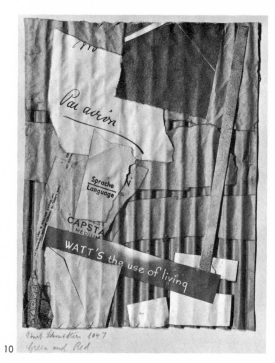

10

11

9. Kurt Schwitters, *Kynast-fest,* 1919.
Sidney Janis Gallery, New York.

10. Kurt Schwitters, *Green and Red,* 1947.
Sidney Janis Gallery, New York.

11. Pablo Picasso, *Glass and Bottle of Suze,* 1913.
Washington University, St. Louis, Missouri.

the acceptance of mass-produced objects, just because they are what is around, not because they issue from idolatrised technology."[10] The source of junk culture is obsolescence, the throwaway material of cities as it collects in drawers, closets, attics, and waste lots. But in contrast to an artist such as Kurt Schwitters, the contemporary artist goes to the limit of the radical implications in using junk. Where Picasso and Schwitters used shreds of real objects that were impregnated with humanity and thus associations of an artistic order, the new artist avoids transformation. He wants his objects to resist incorporation into a smooth aesthetic whole.

The "original status" of the objects which junk artists insist upon obviously can only be maintained if the artist cedes much of his authority to the world of things he is presenting. He is not interpreting, or even re-presenting, but merely presenting. A growing number of commentators regard this as a salubrious development. They are off on a compulsive chase after Reality. As objects multiply, so do mystiques.

Randomness and chance, then, are important values. The composer John Cage, who has elaborated his own techniques based on the laws of chance, applauds the artist Robert Rauschenberg because he makes no pretense at aesthetic selection. (This, of course, is an exaggeration. Rauschenberg is an artist and many of his best works entail considerable transformation, rearrangement and aesthetic selection.) Cage says there is no subject in one of Rauschenberg's combines any more than there is a subject in a page from a newspaper. Rauschenberg himself sees his art as a continuum of bits and parcels from life. There is a hangover from Surrealism in Cage's remark that between Rauschenberg and what he picks up is the quality of encounter.[11] But not the metaphorical encounter of a sewing machine and umbrella on the dissection table—only the chance encounter in the continuum of random sensation we call life.

The acute hunger for realism, which some see as an exacerbated reaction to the ambiguities and uncertainties inherent in abstract painting, is by now a world-

12

12. Robert Rauschenberg, *Coexistence,* 1961.
Leo Castelli Gallery, New York.

13. Robert Rauschenberg, *Wall Street,* 1961.
Collection Ileana Sonnabend.

13

14. Jim Dine, *The White Suit, Self-Portrait,*
Panel I, 1964. Sidney Janis Gallery, New York.
15. Jean Tinguely, *Dissecting Machine,* 1965.
Collection of the artist. Photo Peter Moore.

wide phenomenon, undergoing constant revisions. Two years after he defined junk culture as an acceptance of mass-produced objects, Alloway carried his speculation further. The rejection of metaphor is definite. In an introduction to an exhibition of the work of Jim Dine, Alloway suggested that aesthetic tradition tends to discount the reality of subject matter, stressing art's formality "which can be made a metaphor of ideal order."[12] Such metaphors, he implies, are no longer acceptable.

Dine, who paints huge representations of overcoats with real buttons and shirts with real ties, is giving us not symbols, according to Alloway, but "the object presented as literally and emphatically as possible." In Alloway's triple-play logic, Dine represents overcoats which are overcoats and since we don't expect overcoats which are overcoats from an artist, our surprise is what gives the image value. Furthermore, Alloway now asserts that Dine's use of new objects, "bought fresh," cuts away the fetishistic or social functions of objects.

In this opaque drama in which metaphor is the villain, the diminution of choices is accepted, as was the proliferation of waste, and transformed into an aesthetic principle *faute de mieux.*

The creeping ascendancy of objects so agonizingly sung by Henri Michaux has affected all the arts. The French playwright Ionesco, in his play *The New Tenant,* has used *armoires* to clutter up the stage and eventually to block it off completely as a final curtain. Another French writer, Robbe-Grillet, has made interminable catalogues of objects in his novels in a spirit that he considers realistic. Incidentally, the diminution of choices is seen in Robbe-Grillet's description of his film script *Last Year at Marienbad.* In a plea for what he considers audience participation, he points out that there is no single interpretation of his work and he doesn't wish it to have any decisive form. The spectator can do with it what he likes. The same is true of the machines of Jean Tinguely and the poetry of many of the "beats." The complicity of the audience, invited by the artist, is characteristic of the disillusioned arts of today.

The indisputable novelty of post-war junk art has attracted interest in many circles. An admirable Mexican poet, Octavio Paz, joins in the speculations, writing a catalogue foreword for an exhibition of the Italian

artist Enrico Baj and proffering some disquieting thoughts.[13] Paz, who has been strongly influenced by Surrealism, forces himself beyond his own aesthetic when confronting the furniture pieces of Baj. These chests with warped legs and crazy patterns of *ébénisterie* startle Paz to such a degree that he regards them as a "deep penetration of reality." He notes two steps in Baj's revolt. First he had been concerned in collages to show us that the things we see are also other things. "Just as the poet transforms a commonplace in an image, so Baj employed disparate fragments (mirrors, medals, tapestries) for the creation of strange beings. Poem or collage, in one as in the other, the artist reveals to us what prose or everyday vision conceals: the plurality of reality's meanings." When Baj later came to pieces of furniture, Paz says he first noticed, faithful to his metaphoric methods, their disturbing character: without ceasing to be furniture each piece was a fantastic animal. But, Paz continues, one day they changed back into furniture pieces before his eyes. "Furniture is condemned to be furniture." At this point, Paz goes off into the same mirror palace haunted by Alloway. The grotesque or menacing character of furniture, Paz says, derives not so much from the fact of its seeming to be something else, as from the impossibility of its being something else. "And this is precisely what provides them with their radical alienation, what isolates them from other objects: they are reality-bound, drowned in their own being. There is no metaphorical dimension: they are what they are, their meaning is what they are."

When a serious poet indulges in this agonized appeal for recognition of the real, weaving an exasperated mystique around things as they are, I can only assume that there is a terrifying moral crisis brewing. Paz says that Baj restores to us one of the most perturbing and salutary sensations: that of the identity of things as themselves, in which we must recognize that we are what we are and nothing more. The man-made thing, then, is destined to absorb and nullify the reflections of the poetic mind which, as Paz pointed out, in its metaphoric method indicates the plurality of reality's meanings. Paz' apprehension of furniture as furniture is a long way off from Homer's vision of Achilles' shield.

Although the commentators I mention bravely try to make something positive out of the virtualism practiced by so many artists, the element of whining pathos is never wholly canceled. The fact is that artists presenting objects or sherds and torn fragments often see themselves as traditional victims of the machine age. Their discouragement in the face of avalanches of technocratic advances which reduce the element of human control and make science-fiction nightmares realities is patent in many of their statements. In some ways their gestures are desperate surrenders to chaos.

16. Enrico Baj, *Commode de Style*, 1961.
Galleria Schwarz, Milan. Photo Bacci Attilio.

I said in the beginning that man's relationship to objects does not really change, yet I have traced a pattern which, on the surface of it, appears to show a change. The change, however, is in man's relationship to the cosmos. It is a philosophical change.

The artist, along with other intellectuals, has experienced the revolution of scientific and philosophical thought. It is impossible for him to maintain the classical distance from objects apparent in Homer's writings, just as it is impossible for him to restore the classical unities. Science has swept away the notion of an objective universe, and with it the immovable, resistant entities we call objects. Even so unimaginative a philosopher as the physicist Werner Heisenberg is forced to state—on the basis of his scientific experience—that man confronts himself alone. The subject-object dialectic has been demolished and as yet there has been no philosophic concept adequate to filling the void.

If science, philosophy, and psychology continue to dissolve the exterior world, showing that there is no ultimate indivisible unity, and if objects seem so vastly complex and susceptible to the dissolution bestowed on them by advanced thought, is it any wonder that the artist shares the general crisis? Science dissolves known reality and art attempts to restore it. The preoccupation with objects may be seen as a last-ditch bid of art to resuscitate an objective world. In the wilderness of sub-jectivity that has weighed so heavily on the arts, the artist still seeks the solid materiality, the common-sense verities that seem to have been swallowed up by the radical speculations of science.

We have seen a sequence of reactions since the late nineteenth century. The psychological novel with its fluid stream of consciousness, the role of Freud in both literature and the visual arts, the expression of total flux, are events that have caused profound reactions. In poetry there has been a concerted drive toward concreteness as there has been in the visual arts and music. The word *concrete* itself has come to be a magical antidote. The flight from metaphor, which complicates, is symptomatic. In using objects and trying to deny the nature of the imagination which inevitably allegorizes, poets and painters alike understand that they take a paradoxical position. But, as Paz indicates, it is one of the few positions left for an artist confronted with the shifting shadow world science and philosophy bestow upon us. The unadorned, unworked object, nude and divested of meaning, is one answer to the nonsense dinned in our ears daily (such as slogans: the beer that is real beer, the cigarette that tastes like a cigarette). In a sense, objects in the hands of discouraged artists represent a lament: a lament for the loss of communication, a lament for the loss of the resonance and multiplicity available to an artist such as Homer. —1962.

1. Gustave Flaubert, *Correspondence,* 4 vols., Paris (1893), vol. II, p. 286.

2. These and subsequent references to Apollinaire's writings are taken from *Chroniques d'Art,* Paris, Éditions Gallimard (1960).

3. Jean Cocteau, *Le Secret professionnel,* Paris, Éditions Stock (1922).

4. *The Blind Man,* no. 2 (May, 1917).

5. Marcel Jean, *Histoire de la peinture surréaliste,* Paris Éditions du Seuil (1955).

6. Kurt Schwitters, foreword to 1920 MERZ exhibition, cited in *Dada Painters and Poets,* Willy Verkauf, editor, New York, Wittenborn, Schultz (1951).

7. *Ubu Enchaîné,* Paris, Fasquelle Éditeurs (1953).

8. Allan Kaprow, "Some Observations on Contemporary Art," in *New Forms, New Media I,* catalogue published by the Martha Jackson Gallery, New York (October, 1960).

9. Max Ernst, "Comment on force l'inspiration," in *Le Surréalisme au service de la Révolution* (May, 1933).

10. Lawrence Alloway, "Junk Cultures as Tradition," in *New Forms, New Media, I, op. cit.*

11. John Cage, *Silence,* Middletown, Conn., Wesleyan University Press (1961), pp. 103–108.

12. Lawrence Alloway, mimeographed introduction to an exhibition of the work of Jim Dine held at the Martha Jackson Gallery, New York (1962).

13. Octavio Paz, *Baj, Ebanisterie e mobili,* catalogue published by the Galleria Schwarz, Milan (December, 1961).

FRANÇOISE CHOAY

THE OBJECT AND "REALISM" IN CONTEMPORARY ART

The actual, material, unfigured presence of objects or parts of objects as elements of pictures or sculptures is proving to be one of the characteristics of contemporary art. It began originally with the ready-mades of Marcel Duchamp and the experiments of the Dadaists, and has developed anew in the recent movements named Neo-Dada and Neo-Realism. In this paper I shall attempt to give a semantic analysis of this phenomenon. But the meaning of the concrete object in the artistic scheme of things cannot be elucidated without reference to the meaning of the concrete object in our society, outside of the realm of art.

Francis Ponge[1] calls the dealings we have with our objects a "relationship in the accusative." This role of the object as instigator and shaper is disclosed by historians when they deduce the spiritual culture of a vanished society from the evidence of its material culture, and its mentality from the remains of its everyday objects. Thus we may justifiably think that the appearance of the industrial product, an absolutely new form of object, has not failed to provoke a transformation in Western man. And in fact, technology and industry open a limitless horizon to both man's desires and action which become the "scaffolding" (the *Gestell*) of the world, in Heidegger's analysis.[2] But this enlargement of the human project and this gain in power have as a correlative a completely new mediatization of the object. Efficacity does not take the place of intimacy, and contact is made only at second hand, through the intermediary of a machine.

One extreme example, less obvious than those of the new objects created by mechanization, can stand as a proof of this. The home, the ambiguous place of being and having, the creation of an almost biological wisdom, can become a veritable industrial product in the case of the prefabricated dwelling. Furthermore, the entire domain of building is proving to be industrializable. And this prospect is so accurately felt as a mutation by the constructing conscience that it is giving rise to an instinctive or critical reaction. This is historically an original phenomenon, which came into being at the end of the last century, and which, from Gaudi and Guimard to Frederick Kiesler by way of certain of Le Corbusier's realizations, could be called *poetic architecture:* the utilitarian function is obliterated by hedonist-plastic considerations; the dwelling-place becomes sculpture.

Thus the mediatization of the relationship of the object to the human subject constitutes a fundamental differential character of this new object, the industrial product. But the industrial product can also take on another character, contingent and subsidiary, when it gives rise to concerted formal and scientific research joined to an aesthetic conception. We have been too preoccupied with relating the work of industrial design to the craft tradition to emphasize its absolute novelty. Until Ruskin's formulation of the problem, which was itself dialectically linked with the development of mechanics, the question of the beauty of the common object was formulated differently. It was, in fact, either lived as an existential value in the case of popular art, or else it was integrated into the formal system of a style. When, after the misgivings raised by Ruskin, the first theoreticians of industrial design asked themselves how to conserve in objects created by industry an intrinsic

beauty which would replace the lost beauty of individual handwork, the very posing of the problem was a revolutionary development in the tradition of Western art, a development created by the dichotomy between the value of use and the value of representation. The picture takes its aesthetic value from its abstract function of representation which de-realizes the object represented. This is why the picture is not a thing and why history has transferred it from its original place as idol, that is, from the altar to the easel.

In this perspective the exemplary research of the Bauhaus suddenly emerges as a scandal. A significant fact is the collusion of this group and its homologues with Cubism. We may in fact assume that Cubism is a belated stage on the way to de-realization: a stage where the object becomes transparent, reducible to a simple geometrical system, its truth expressible in two dimensions. The generation of Constructivists and rationalist architects after World War I took up these plastic principles again to apply them to products already mediatized by industry and which thus undergo a double de-realization. (These remarks are not valid only insofar as Cubism is concerned, but also for any "aesthetization" which has as its point of departure a system of figurative values external to the essence of the object.) Thus the industrial designers, wishing to reply to the objections raised by Ruskin, contributed even further to transforming the nature of the everyday object. The quest for what we must call a "universal style," applicable to the abstract products of industry, leads them to reconstruct these products according to the abstract values of a figured style.

The preceding remarks permit one to situate the position of Marcel Duchamp, who represents a kind of absolute historical departure for reflections on the object and the relation between art and the object in an industrial society. What, in fact, is a *ready-made* if not a cluster of often contradictory affirmations and negations? It is first of all the negation of a figured art (figurative or not) which appropriates the object by an intellectual process: Duchamp previously developed to their extreme the analytical and synthetic possibilities of Cubism, and having profited from this radical experimentation, he confronts the unreality of representation with the weight of the real and of the critical conscience. The reverse of negation is thus an affirmation which offers the contemplator a strange object in which he will look in vain for any trace of craftsmanship. In reality Duchamp's intention is twofold, derision and exaltation at the same time, and this ambiguity constitutes the fertile core of his work. On one hand, the industrial product is denounced in all its anonymity, its banality, its essential poverty which deprives it of human and poetic qualities. On the other hand, it still remains an object which a simple decision on the part of the spectator can extract from its context to give it mystery and opacity. The solution of the alternative is based ultimately on intentionality: the ready-made is satire, but at the same time it is also a proposition of ascesis and conversion. And this proposition, so aridly formulated with the nakedness of theory, was to open up fertile and less austere paths.

In fact, while one current in contemporary art perseveres in an intellectual appropriation (be it of the

1. Marcel Duchamp, *Why not sneeze?*
Galleria Schwarz, Milan. Photo Bacci Attilio.

external world through ever more allusive schematization, or be it of the emotional world through the figured exorcism of its unavowed or unconscious phantasms), for another group of present-day artists paintings and sculptures are no longer representations (representational or not, it hardly matters) but objects. And these *useless* objects of the artist can only take on meaning when reintegrated into the dialectics of industrial society which opposes them to the *handsome* products of industrial design.

The contemporary artist's "Copernican" conversion to the object presents a number of modalities which it is important to situate in relation to one another in order to seek out the semantic implications. First of all, one can distinguish two kinds of objects which correspond to two kinds of attitudes: in one, elements of the external world are transferred from their habitual context to another level where they are assigned an aesthetic function; in the other we witness a real manufacturing process but deprived of any utilitarian function. The first is thus more mental than the second and the artist's material participation is more limited, since it can tend toward passivity in cases where the work consists in nothing more than a simple choice, a mere decision. Things raised to the power of *objets d'art* are, depending on the artist, borrowed from the domain of nature or from that of culture. Jean Dubuffet, for instance, has with incomparable skill made these two worlds "interfere" in an ambiguous achievement which I mention here as a kind of introduction to a movement with which it is not to be confused. Dubuffet's work is actually composed of two kinds of "pictures": graffiti (comparable to those which the popular hand traces on the walls of our cities) or simple materials or collages (comparable to more or less differentiated patches of earth or clods of turf). The object, then, is not present in either of these instances. This is rather a case of an art which depicts, but with the aim of obtaining an *analogon* which is invested with a double function: to rehabilitate and to "present" realities (cultural ones like graffiti or natural ones like the bits of earth) considered trivial or absolutely banal, and then to make these doubles perform like the objects themselves.

2. Jean Dubuffet, *The Internal Life of the Mineral,* 1960. Metal foil on composition board. Collection of the artist.

But the complexity of Dubuffet's work arises in part from the fact that he does not abandon craftsmanship nor the process of depicture. The method of artists who have totally forsaken the simulacrum in favor of the object alone is simpler. One may define it in terms of the importance of the transformations worked on the raw material by the "creator." The simplest level consists, then, in the simple choice of an element represented in its nakedness: such is the case with the torn posters invented by Raymond Hains, Mimmo Rotella, Jacques de Villeglé; such too with the roots and pebbles which John Baxter or Etienne Martin have taught us to appreciate. But the human hand may intervene to work transformations—often, moreover, anthropomorphic transformations. This would be the case with the "Figures of Precarious Life" created by Dubuffet out of cork or coal, or again Karel Appel's tree roots painted so that they turn into fantastic monsters. Finally, the selection of objects can tend toward a complex composition, as in the work of all the Neo-Realists or Neo-Dadaists. Here and there one may note the importance of the sordid as an inductor of reality. But the problem of the organization of ensembles almost always reintroduces an aesthetization according to the classical rules of representation: this is particularly clear in the case of Robert Rauschenberg. In another connection a polemical intention frequently influences the choice of elements: French Neo-Realism, when it ceases to indulge exclusively in practical jokes (significant as such), tends to derision and irony; in the United States, on the other hand, we find a less mediatized violence in criticism:

the best example might be that proposed by John Chamberlain with his pieces of old iron which cry out the tragic absurdity of man in the machine age. Finally, we must end this brief inventory with the images of Pierre Bettencourt, in which he uses unprepared natural materials to embody very realistically drawn dream-like scenes. Eggshells, sea-shells, grains of corn take on new reality by suddenly being torn out of context. Here we are at the opposite pole from Dubuffet: the image is completely dissociated from the objects; the objects, intact, play their roles autonomously, even though their presence may ultimately contribute to transform the picture, which ceases to be limited to its representational function alone. The common characteristic of the highly diverse works mentioned here resides in the effective presence of the material world, substituted for its image, and having a direct, not mediatized effect on the senses.

But art may also become object through mere fabrication, without reference to the reality of the senses. In that case there is a kind of exaltation of the object as a sacred repository of the human gesture. The spirit of this tendency, in its opposition to classical abstract art, was defined before it happened by Rimbaud when he wrote in *A Season in Hell:* "I found the famous figures in modern painting and poetry ridiculous. I preferred stupid paintings, the panels over doors, stage sets, circus booths, signs, cheap colored prints . . ." The whole arsenal of *art brut* is already invoked here: the touching ponderousness of the human project in its most naïve or maladroit materializations.

3

4

5. Étienne Martin, *Demure Opéra or Demure No. 9,* 1964.
Acacia wood. Photo André Morain.
6. Jean Dubuffet, *Figure of Precarious Life:
The Ragged One,* 1954. Collection Mr. and Mrs. Gordon Bunshaft.

7. Jean Dubuffet, *Figure of Precarious Life: Saimiri*, 1954.
8. Karel Appel, *Tête blanche partout*, 1961. Painted olive wood. Photo Augustin Dumage.

7   8

9. Robert Rauschenberg, *Winter Pool*, 1959.
Collection Mr. and Mrs. Victor Ganz. Photo Rudolph Burckhardt.

10. John Chamberlain, *Mozo*, 1962. Welded automobile metals.
Leo Castelli Gallery, New York. Photo Rudolph Burckhardt.

11. Pierre Bettencourt, *La Bouchée*, 1963.

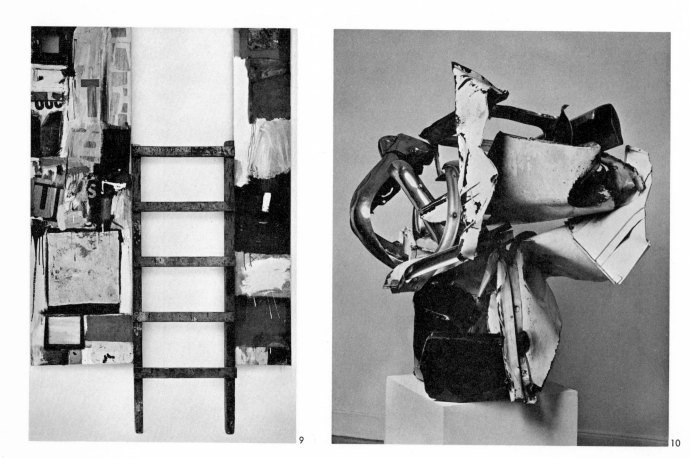

9

10

11

12. Alberto Burri, *Composition 8,* 1953. Collage of burlap, sand, and thread. Museum of Modern Art, New York. Mr. and Mrs. David M. Solinger Fund. Photo Soichi Sunami.

13. Zoltán Kemeny, *Association of Two Optics,* 1962. Copper and white iron. Collection Bo Boustedt. Photo Walter Dräyer.

But the domain of *art brut* remains nonetheless in ambivalence, since its creations were originally images for the naïve mentality before becoming objects for the reflective and contemplative conscience. A first consciously directed step toward the transformation of painting into object may be represented by the canvases of Antoni Tapies or Alberto Burri. Paint in the works of these artists is replaced by materials like cement or burlap; painting by seams, rents, or simple imprints. We are not face to face with objects but with ambiguous things which are now neither images nor symbols. Certainly we are confronted with tearings and surgings and some might claim that they are symbolic; but a symbol is always figurative, whereas in these works we have not the image of a wound but the wound itself, and it is precisely this ontological aim which allows us to invoke the proximity of the object.

At a second stage the object already affirms itself without ambiguity in reliefs such as those of Zoltán Kemeny or Alfonso Ossorio. These are true objects which celebrate the creative gift of man, with a corresponding lyricism, but in a different key where delirium, irony, and nostalgia participate to different degrees.

At a final level, the object at last detaches itself from the wall, loses any reference to its former state as a pic-ture, and unfurls its three-dimensionality in space. It is here that the recent privilege of sculpture among the visual arts appears most clearly. Today it multiplies its fantastic creations: these are, on the one hand, useless machines or pseudo-machines, charged with humor and satirical inventiveness, like those of Richard Stankiewicz and Jean Tinguely; on the other hand, pseudo-idols or totems like the sculptures of Robert Muller. These examples, however, remain charged with reminiscences and allusions, but our age has also created a category of objects which function independent of any direct reference to the forms of the past. I am thinking of the meticulous boxes of Joseph Cornell or again of those boxes inside which Bernard Requichot has superimposed and jumbled together frantic coils of painting. But even more I am thinking of the monochrome constructions of Louise Nevelson in which the object is presented explicitly in its opacity and its mystery; where, among doors which open upon nothing, the object appears as a contradictory place of emptiness and plenitude, the temptation of an endless dialogue, trap for desires and intentions, and where, finally, the dimension of history is present only through the mediation of irony and a tender derision.

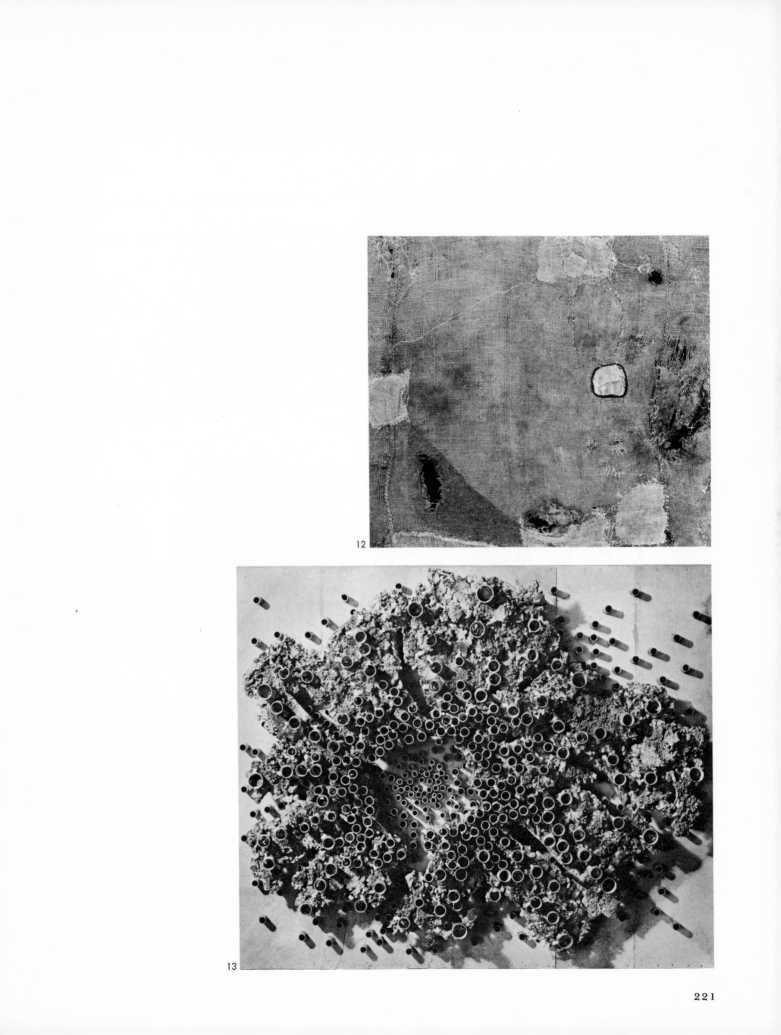

12

13

14. Robert Muller, *Ex Voto,* 1957. Forged iron.
Museum of Modern Art, New York. Philip C. Johnson Fund.
Photo Soichi Sunami.

15. Jean Tinguely, *Motor Cocktail,* 1965.
Alexander Iolas Gallery, New York.

16. Bernard Requichot. *Reliquary with Peacock
Feathers,* 1955–1956. Photo Jean-Pierre Sudre.

15

15

16

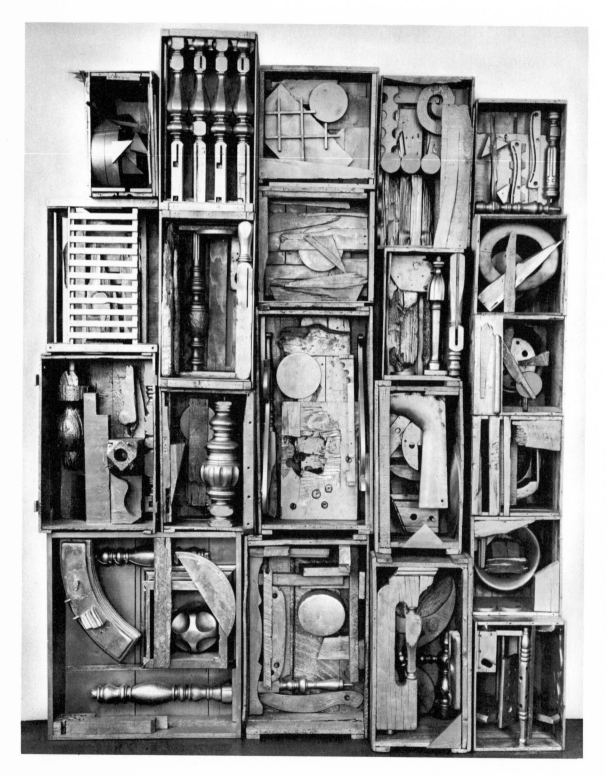

224

17. Louise Nevelson, *Royal Tide V*. Gilded wood.
Photo Rudolph Burckhardt.

So ends a brief review which has attempted simply to show the diversity and richness of the object as a form of art, not industrial, in an industrial society. Certainly it is an extremely limited field since it takes up but a fraction of the marginal area which art occupies in our society. But it is interesting nevertheless to look for the meaning of this contemporary movement which we might call *realism* (or even *objectism*) in order to contrast it with the unreality of all representational, imaged forms, whether they be abstract or even naïvely faithful to socialized perception such as conceived by "Socialist realism." The preceding analysis, then, points to a dissatisfaction on the part of a fraction of today's artists concerning their relation to the world. Art no longer has as its goal the task of rendering the world transparent; science is completing a take-over of the intellect, and technology is surrounding us with objects de-realized through multiplied mediations. The effort at dis-alienation in the face of the technical object, such as that attempted by Gilbert Simondon,[3] remains on a strictly intellectual level.

In brief, plastic creation has stumbled on a difficulty comparable to that encountered by philosophical reflection when it seeks to find again *"die Sachen selbst."* But this movement of conversion to the object itself, to the detriment of its image, is accomplished according to two temporal vectors oriented in opposite directions, and this pro- and retroversive motivation indeed at times appears simultaneously in a single work. On one hand, the polarization of the artist toward the object can be due to a nostalgic reaching toward the past: moved by an almost mystic mentality, contemporary man re-grets and tries to find again the mechanisms of fascination which delight him in ethnological descriptions. The object is invested with a magic power and the terminology used by a mind as keen as Dubuffet's lets hardly any ambiguity subsist as regards the efficacity of the work. It is certain, nevertheless, that the critical conscience prevents the complete success of the enterprise, and always implies a margin of irony, an appeal to the spectator's complicity. On the other hand, the vector of the artist may be oriented toward the future, and the historical situation of the world may be taken over by a polemical and satirical conscience. In these cases we may even get ambiguous and difficult attempts where the painters or sculptors seem to give themselves the task of affirming the presence of the object, subtracted from both the alienation of desire and the de-realization of conceiving. This is a double movement of naturalization and humanization. And when the contemporary artist presents us with a rock or a root as an object of art or a mass of old iron as the incarnation of a biological kind of creation, it does indeed seem as though we might see therein a Utopian undertaking which would like to choose itself as shaper of the world of tomorrow. In this sense, contemporary realism or objectism would be faithful to the protensive vocation of Western art.   — 1962

1. In preface to catalogue, *Antagonisme II, L'Object,* Pavillon de Marsan (1962).
2. Martin Heidegger, "Die Frage der Technik" in *Vorträge und Aufsätze,* Pfullingen (1954).
3. *Du mode d'existence des objects techniques,* Paris (1958).

Christopher Alexander Architect and mathematician. Born Vienna, 1936. Studied at Trinity College, Cambridge, and Harvard University. Now working at the University of California, Berkeley. Interested in all aspects of form: the creation, description, classification, nature, function, and behavior of all kinds of spatial organization, and the use of this knowledge to create new forms of spatial organization for the environment. Author: *Notes on the Synthesis of Form* (1964); and co-author (with Serge Chermayeff), *Community and Privacy: Toward a New Architecture of Humanism* (1963).

Dore Ashton Art critic. Born Newark, New Jersey, 1928. Studied at University of Wisconsin, The New School for Social Research, New York, and Radcliffe College. Teaches at the School of Visual Arts, New York. Most active as writer and critic. Associate editor, *The Art Digest*, 1950–54. Associate art critic, *New York Times*, 1955–. Art critic, *Art and Architecture*, 1955–. Author: *Abstract Art Before Columbus* (1957); *Philip Guston* (1959); *Unknown Shore: A View of Contemporary Art* (1962). Presently completing a book on the assumptions of modern art and preparing another on American sculpture.

Michael J. Blee Architect. Born Brighton, England, 1931. Associate ARIBA, since 1953. Practiced in Singapore and Ceylon; traveled extensively in Japan, India, Afghanistan. Master's Degree, M.I.T., under Gyorgy Kepes. Worked with Architects Collaborative, Cambridge, Mass., and Sir Basil Spence, London, before going into private practice. Lecturer in Department of Architecture, Brighton. Research in color in Greece, which is now second home. Particular interest in environmental structure of primitive communities. Current work: church on Thames, a community center, and miscellaneous interior design projects. Articles in *Architectural Review*, and *Landscape*.

Marcel Breuer Architect and designer. Born Pécs, Hungary, 1902. 1920–28: studied and taught at the Bauhaus. Pioneer in the early 20's and 30's in the field of furniture design utilizing bent tubular steel, aluminum, and plywood. 1935–37: in England, important work in both furniture and architectural design. 1937–46: taught at Graduate School of Design, Harvard University, and, in partnership with Walter Gropius, carried on private architectural practice. Since 1946, private architectural practice, office in New York City. Important architectural contributions, particularly in the area of domestic architecture and academic buildings. Among the innumerable examples of his domestic architecture: the Harnischmacher House, Wiesbaden (1932) and the Robinson House, Williamstown, Mass. (1946). Outstanding among recent public works: UNESCO Headquarters, Paris, in collaboration with Nervi and Zehrfuss (1958).

Theodore M. Brown Architectural historian. Born Massachusetts, 1925. Trained as architect, M.I.T., and as art historian, Harvard University and University of Utrecht, The Netherlands. Since 1958, Assistant and Associate Professor, University of Louisville. Major publication: *The Work of G. Rietveld, Architect* (1958).

Françoise Choay   Aesthetician and writer on art and architecture. Born Paris, 1925. Presently preparing thesis on some philosophical problems raised by town planning. Most active as collaborator with various newspapers, art and architecture magazines: art and architecture column in *France Observateur*, 1956–60; architecture editor *L'Oeil*, 1957–60; special number on architecture, *Revue d'Esthétique*, 1963; *Art International*, Paris editor since 1960. Author of: *L'UNESCO, Le Corbusier, Mark Tobey*, and a most recent work, *Urbanisme, Utopis et Realites*, published in 1965.

Gillo Dorfles   Aesthetician and art critic. Born Trieste, 1910. Professor of Aesthetics, University of Milan. Former editor of *Aut Aut* and *Domus*. Has lectured widely in Europe and America. Major publications: *Discorso tecnico delle arti* (1950); *Barocco nell'architettura moderna* (1951); *Le oscillazioni del gusto* (1958); *Divenire delle arti* (1959); *L'architettura moderna* (1954 and 1962); *Ultime tendenze dell'arte* (1961); *Simbolo, Comunicazione, Consumo* (1962); *Il Disegno industriale e la sua estetica* (1963); *Nuovi riti, nuovi miti* (1965).

Kazuhiko Egawa   Art critic and teacher. Born Tokyo, Japan, 1896. Studied philosophy and history of the fine arts at Waseda University. Now Professor of Design Theory at the Musashino Art University, Tokyo. Since 1950 he has been member of the Tokyo Study Group on Modern Art and Design. For this body he has given many lectures on the *Language of Vision* and *The New Landscape in Art and Science* by Gyorgy Kepes, as well as on *Vision in Motion* and *New Vision* by Moholy-Nagy.

Joan M. Erikson   Designer, craftsman, educator. Studied at Teacher's College, Columbia University, and sociology at University of Pennsylvania. Jewelry exhibited in a number of museums and in the 1963 traveling exhibit of the Museum of Contemporary Crafts, N.Y. Director for a number of years of the Activities Program, Austin Riggs Center for Research and the Treatment of Neuroses, Stockbridge, Mass. Co-organizer of the Diablo Valley Arts and Crafts Association in California and the Berkshire Arts Center, Mass. Writings: "Nothing to Fear: Notes on the Life of Eleanor Roosevelt," *Daedalus*, 1964; *The Cloth of the Mother Goddess*, in preparation at Indian Institute of Design, Ahmedabad, India. The present article is based on an unpublished book, *The Ubiquitous Bead*.

Jean Hélion   Painter. Born Couterne, Normandy, 1904. Began painting in Paris in the early 20's. 1929: exhibited first abstract works; founded with Van Doesburg and others the group and review *Art Concret*. 1930: founded with Arp, Delaunay, Kupka and others the group and magazine *Abstraction-Creation*. 1936: moved to United States. 1937: took part in London Gallery exhibition "Constructive Art" arranged by *Circle*. After 1939 returned to figurative painting. 1940: in French army. 1942: returned to United States; wrote *They Shall Not Have Me*, record of war experiences. Since 1946 has lived in Paris, traveling widely in Europe and spending summers in Belle-Ile. Innumerable exhibitions throughout Europe and in United States. 1964: retrospective exhibition, Gallery of Modern Art, New York. Works in permanent collections, including: Musée d'Art Moderne, Paris; The Tate Gallery, London; Museum of Modern Art and Guggenheim Museum, New York City; and Art Institute of Chicago.

Gyorgy Kepes	Painter and designer. Born Selyp, Hungary, 1906. 1930–36: worked in Berlin and London on film, stage, and exhibition design. In 1937 came to the United States to head the Light and Color Department, Institute of Design, Chicago. Since 1946 Professor of Visual Design, M.I.T. Author: *Language of Vision; The New Landscape in Art and Science*. Editor of *The Visual Arts Today*. Most active as painter. His works are in the permanent collections of many museums, including: Albright Knox Art Gallery, Buffalo; Museum of Fine Arts, Boston; Museum of Fine Arts, Houston; Museum of Modern Art, New York; Museum of Art, San Francisco; Whitney Museum, New York.
Marshall McLuhan	University professor and author of important works on communication. Born Edmonton, Canada, 1911. Studied at University of Manitoba and Cambridge University. Taught at Universities of Wisconsin, and St. Louis, Assumption University, and University of Toronto where since 1952 he has been Full Professor. Co-editor of *Explorations Magazine*, 1954–59. Director of Media Project for National Association of Educational Broadcasters and U.S. Office of Education, 1956–60. Appointment in 1963 by President of Toronto University to create new Center for Culture and Technology (psychic and social consequences of technologies and media). Frequent appearances on TV and lecture platform. Contributor to many journals in the field of literature. Author: *The Mechanical Bride; Folklore of Industrial Man* (1951); (with E. S. Carpenter) *Explorations in Communications* (1960); *The Gutenberg Galaxy: The Making of Typographic Man* (1962); *Understanding Media* (1964).
Sir Herbert Read	Poet and critic of art and literature. Born Yorkshire, England, 1893. Studied at University of Leeds. After World War I held various civil posts, including service at Victoria and Albert Museum. 1931: became Professor of Fine Arts, University of Edinburgh. 1929–30: Clark Lecturer, Trinity College, Cambridge. 1935–36: Sydney Jones Lecturer in Art, University of Liverpool. 1953–54: Charles Eliot Norton Professor of Poetry, Harvard University. Knighted in 1953. 1933–38: Editor of *The Burlington Magazine*. 1939–64: editorial director of publishing firm. Author: *Collected Poems, Reason and Romanticism, Wordsworth, In Defence of Shelley, The Meaning of Art, Art and Society, Art and Industry, Poetry and Anarchism, Education Through Art, Phases of English Poetry, The True Voice of Feeling, Icon and Idea, The Art of Sculpture, A Concise History of Modern Painting, A Concise History of Modern Sculpture, The Form of Things Unknown, A Letter to a Young Painter, To Hell with Culture,* and *The Contrary Experience* (autobiography). Book entitled *The Origins of Form in Art* to be published in 1966.
Leonardo Ricci	Born Rome, 1918. Professor of Architectural Design and Visual Design, University of Florence. Director, Institutes of Architectural Design and Town Planning, University of Florence. President, Tuscan-Umbrian Section, The National Institute of Town Planning. Visiting Professor, M.I.T., 1960, and Pennsylvania State University, 1965. Major architectural works in Italy: Mercato dei Fiori, Pescia; Villaggio Monterinaldi, Florence; Quartiere populare, Sòrgane, Florence; Centro Direzionale per aree depresse, Villaggio Monte degli Ulivi, Riesi, Sicily; Quartiere Sperimentale, Granarolo, Genoa. Contributor to many architectural reviews and author of the book *Anonymous 20th Century* (1962).

Henry S. Stone, Jr.   Born 1942, Corpus Christi, Texas. Student, Social Relations Department, Harvard University. Presently working towards Ph.D. Plans to combine practice as psychotherapist with research in personality, emphasizing work with adolescents in both areas. Has worked on documentary films in Film Study Center, Carpenter Center for the Visual Arts, Harvard University, and is presently teaching assistant for beginning film course and freshman seminar in film. Has an empathy for motorcyclists, with whom he has associated for some years, and has himself done a good deal of motorcycle riding.

Frederick S. Wight   Museum director, painter, writer. Born New York City, 1902. Studied at University of Virginia and Harvard University. Formerly, Associate Director, Institute of Contemporary Art, Boston. Now Director of Art Galleries and Professor of Art, University of California, Los Angeles. Organized major traveling exhibitions, including those showing works of Le Corbusier, Gropius, Orozco, Sheeler, Marin, Graves, Hofmann, Tomlin, Neutra, Dove, and Modigliani. His own paintings exhibited in numerous one-man shows in New York City, California, and New Mexico. Author: *Van Gogh* (1953); *Goya* (1954). Co-author: *New Art in America* (1957); *Looking at Modern Art* (1957). Has also written numerous novels, including a fictionalized biography of Modigliani.

Designed by the arts staff, George Braziller, Inc.
Printed in offset by Connecticut Printers, Inc., Hartford, Conn.